The Etruscans

The Emergence of Man

The Etruscans

by Dora Jane Hamblin
and the Editors
of TIME-LIFE BOOKS

TIME-LIFE BOOKS

New York

The Author: DORA JANE HAMBLIN, who also wrote *The First Cities* and a section of *Life Before Man* in this series, is a freelance writer who now lives in Etruscan country, on Lake Bracciano, Italy. For many years a member of the LIFE staff, she has also written *Pots and Robbers,* about Etruscan tombs and the *tombaroli,* or tomb thieves; *Buried Cities and Ancient Treasures,* about archeology in Turkey; and *The Appian Way, a Journey.*

The Consultants: LARISSA BONFANTE WARREN, a Classicist and archeologist, is on the faculty of the New York University and a foreign member of the Institute for Etruscan and Italic Studies in Florence. She has written a book entitled *Etruscan Dress,* and is co-author of a forthcoming volume on Greek and Roman dress. ELLEN KOHLER, a specialist in Etruscan religion on the faculty of the University of Pennsylvania, gave special assistance on the fourth chapter of this book.

Editorial Associate: ANN NATANSON, TIME-LIFE BOOKS' correspondent in Rome since 1964, contributed indispensable research for the illustrations and text of this volume.

The Cover: Seated in a two-wheeled wooden cart driven by a servant, a well-to-do Etruscan couple enjoys an outing near Sovana, in central Italy. They are dressed according to Fourth Century B.C. fashion, in clothing of fine wool decorated along the edges with patterns of contrasting colors. The woman wears a golden diadem and a mantle over her hair. In this scene, painted on a photograph of an Etruscan-built road that is still in use today, artist Michael Hampshire has captured a dominant and moving aspect of Etruscan life —the affectionate ties that bound husband and wife together.

Contents

Introduction

The Etruscans present one of history's most fascinating problems. Beyond the specialized world of scholars, a penumbra of mystery has been created around this extraordinary people that cannot fail to arouse the curiosity of everyone who contemplates them; and indeed, their story has come down to us cloaked in speculation and legend.

How is it that so many questions are posed about a people who lived in a period about which we know such a great deal? Their civilization rose, flowered and declined at the center of the Classical world: at the very gates of Rome. The fortunes of that city are amply documented, as are those of Greece and Carthage—neighbors and contemporaries of Rome and Etruria. But a comprehensive chronicle of the Etruscans' history is missing from the annals of the ancient world. If they catalogued their own times, that record has been irrevocably lost.

Unique aspects of the Etruscans' historical development—particularly their precocious and rapid rise, and their equally swift decline—may account for the absence of documentation. Furthermore, this was a people who pursued their lives with a clear preference for action over introspection.

Their civilization acquired its mysterious aura early in its own time. Roman historians, writing only a few centuries after the fact, already looked on the intense and ephemeral experience of this ebullient, adventurous and gifted people as strange, alien and semilegendary. Despite the great influence of Greek civilization and culture on Etruria, primitive elements persisted in the Etruscans' outlook on life and in their religion, funeral customs and even in their language, whose basic structure seems to be linked in origin with the most remote, ancient pre-Indo-European tongues of western Asia and the Mediterranean. That archaic stamp survived ineradicably until Etruria had been completely absorbed into the unity of Roman Italy. No wonder the Etruscans present so many problems to 20th Century scholarship.

Within the past 200 years, the rhythm of Etruscan discoveries and excavations has quickened. Many important finds have enriched Italy's museums, as well as those of Europe and America. Archeological discoveries made in Etruria itself, and in territories dominated or influenced by the Etruscans, have contributed to a growing storehouse of knowledge. It is at last becoming possible to see, with increasing clarity, how the people of Etruria achieved their high standard of living and their technical expertise; how they planned and built their cities, cemeteries, temples, fortifications and roads; how they organized their use of land; how they achieved mastery in the fields of painting, sculpture and jewelry; how they ate, slept, dressed and played.

It is likely that the resources of modern technology —ranging from aerial photography to sophisticated dating techniques—will continue to help sharpen the blurred outlines of the Etruscan way of life. For the time being, the most important problem is to progress beyond the old-fashioned, fragmentary approach to study and research—wherein each discipline pursues its own methods—and coordinate the traditional roles of archeologists, historians and linguists. Only with the closest possible collaboration among the various disciplines can scholars reach the most advantageous position from which to attempt a unified, authentic historical interpretation of the Etruscan world.

In my own work, I have been fortunate enough to be able to pursue the archeological study of Etruscan places and objects within a promising and increasingly exciting historical framework. At Pyrgi, for instance, were found the remains of two large temples and their elaborate, figured terra-cotta decorations, along with the earliest written source of Italian history. The latter is embodied in three gold tablets inscribed in the Phoenician and Etruscan languages. The tablets, I believe, contribute invaluable information about Etruscan political and religious institutions, and about the relationship between the peoples of Etruria and Carthage at the beginning of the Fifth Century B.C. That period marked the last era of success and prosperity before the Etruscans began their centuries-long glide into oblivion.

For me, it was truly an extraordinary and moving experience to open and read the tablets. It is to be hoped that we may have similar experiences in the future, since it is more than probable that the soil of Etruria reserves many other such surprises for us.

Massimo Pallottino
Professor of Etruscan and Italic Studies
University of Rome

Chapter One: The Enduring Smile

Just north of Rome, between the Tyrrhenian Sea and the western slopes of the Apennine Mountains, lies a tumultuous landscape of sudden brown cliffs and dark green *macchia*—a scrubby underbrush of scrawny oak, tangled wild fig, purple-topped thistle and chestnut trees. Here in prehistoric times eruptions blew the tops off volcanoes, creating the lakes of Bracciano, Vico and Bolsena, and depositing debris everywhere. Some of the detritus was the dense, dark basalt the Romans would one day use to build such roads as the Appian Way. Some was reddish-brown volcanic tufa, a soft and porous stone.

Millennia of torrential winter rains turned streams into temporary rivers that carved the unresisting tufa into crags and plateaus, with shapes like beached ships and landlocked islands. Rivulets seamed the landscape like an old peasant's weather-beaten face.

In late winter in this region the bright yellow blossoms of mimosa trees fringe the crevices; in spring the countryside catches fire with the scarlet of wild poppies; in autumn the scene mellows with the gold of broom. In summer the land is sere, except for the thin green lines of the sculpting streams. The sun casts the sheer sides of the tufa scarps into light and shadow, and bounces back and forth from the twin blues of sky and lake as though in a hall of mirrors.

To the north lies beguiling Tuscany, a land of wide alluvial valleys, its slopes quilted with the patterns of vineyards and punctuated by rows of dark cypress

The painted terra-cotta head of a warrior, eyes hooded and lips curved in an arrogant smile, bespeaks the supreme confidence of the Etruscans at the peak of their military might. His mustache is trimmed to fit the visorless helmet framing his brow. The head is all that survives of this life-sized statue, which probably stood in a temple in the Fifth Century B.C.

trees. Tuscany is the region of Italy's celebrated hill towns, clinging like lichen to rocky peaks as high as 2,000 feet. Toward the Tyrrhenian Sea the landscape rolls out onto flatlands, low-lying fields broken by high, rocky outcrops that stand with their heads near the clouds and their feet in the waves.

All this was Etruscan country. For six and a half centuries, from 750 B.C. to 100 B.C.—beginning when Rome was still little more than a cluster of huts—this region was the heartland of the people who built Italy's first great civilization. "Etruria filled the whole length of Italy with the noise of her name," recalled the Roman historian Livy, writing around the time of Christ. At the peak of their power, from 600 B.C. to 500 B.C., Etruscans dominated or influenced all northern Italy from south of Venice on the Adriatic to the Tyrrhenian Sea, including much of the Po Valley, the entire center of the peninsula from the Apennines westward, to the nearest islands off the Tyrrhenian shore. Long before Livy's day any political seer gazing ahead would have predicted that this land was destined to be called not Rome but Etruria.

The emergence of Etruscan civilization around 750 B.C. was very sudden compared to the crawling pace of most changes in prehistory. Seemingly all at once, among and around the primitive hamlets that prehistoric settlers had sprinkled over central Italy, there appeared a people who built cities instead of villages. They knew how to write, and did so in an alphabet borrowed from the Greeks. But they wrote and spoke in a language unlike any other in the ancient world.

They were sailors, warriors, merchants. Their skilled miners exploited Italy's mineral resources, enabling their merchants to deal in raw copper, lead and iron, and finished metalwork. They traded vigorously with Greece, with Greek colonies to the south and in Sicily and Ionia, with cities in the far eastern Mediterranean and Phoenician ports in northern Africa, Cyprus and Spain. They lived as exuberant sybarites, banqueting sumptuously, waited upon by crowds of servants and slaves, surrounded by luxury. Their aristocratic dead were buried in elaborately carved and painted stone tombs. Gifted artists and craftsmen, they made sculptures of themselves and of their gods in terra cotta, in bronze and in stone. As metalsmiths, they fashioned weapons and utensils of bronze and iron, and elegant gold jewelry.

The Greeks called them Tyrrhenoi or Tyrsenoi; the name survives to identify the sea that bordered their land to the west. To the Romans, who wrote much about them, they were the Tusci or Etrusci; Tuscany still echoes this name. They called themselves Rasenna or Rasna, so the Romans reported.

The Etruscan names for the cities they built have been lost with time and most of the sites are today best remembered as the Romans knew them: Tarquinii, Caere, Vulci, Veii, Clusium (see page 14). Their other urban centers are most often identified by the modern Italian names: Orvieto, Arezzo, Cortona, Fiesole, Volterra. The Etruscan vestiges of these ancient towns, which provided the foundations for later occupants, were long ago buried or destroyed, and the treasures recovered from the ruins have been scattered to the museums of the world. But the Etruscans still live on the lips of all who speak of Italy.

Their cities provided an indispensable link between the already highly developed cultures of the eastern Mediterranean and the primitive tribes that were to become mighty Rome. They transformed

An Etruscan Chronology

c. 900 B.C.
Villanovans living on sites ultimately developed as cities by the Etruscans.
753 B.C.
Traditional date for founding of Rome by Romulus.
c. 750 B.C.
First Etruscan cities rise. Greeks establish trading colonies in southern Italy and Sicily.
c. 650 B.C.
Expansion from nuclear settlements to areas south of Rome.
616 B.C.
First Etruscan, Lucius Tarquinius, ascends Roman throne.
c. 600 B.C.
Height of power. Allied Etruscan and Carthaginian navies hold sway over western Mediterranean. Founding of Capua and further expansion of power south toward environs of modern Salerno.
c. 550 B.C.
Greek religious pantheon modified and adopted; first temples built. Expansion into the Po Valley.
c. 535 B.C.
Naval victory over Greeks provides dominion over Corsica.
474 B.C.
Control of western Mediterranean lost after defeat by Syracusan Greeks in naval battle off Cumae.
396 B.C.
Veii conquered after 10-year siege by Rome.
c. 390 B.C.
Gauls sack Rome.
358-265 B.C.
Piecemeal Roman conquest of Etruria.
280 B.C.
Leading Etruscan cities undertake alliances with Rome.
218-202 B.C.
Etruria supports Rome against Carthage during Second Punic War, won by Romans.
c. 125 B.C.
Peasants driven from small farms and conscripted into the Roman legions.
87 B.C.
Under the *Lex Julia*, Etruscans assume privileges and obligations of full Roman citizenship.

Rome into a city and started it on its way to becoming an empire. And without Roman imperialism the history of the West would have been quite different.

For all the power and wealth they achieved, however, the Etruscans were a paradox. The ancients never completely understood them, nor can modern scholars. They had the potential to dominate their world, but they frittered away their power in rivalries between competing cities, unable to make common cause against any common enemy—whether Greece or Rome or barbarian tribes.

The Etruscans' entry into recorded history came at a time when the Mediterranean world was emerging from a series of upheavals followed by a period of quiet that lasted almost 400 years. Since the 12th Century B.C. the great powers of the Near East had been in decline. Egypt had suffered several stunning blows by invaders identified as the Peoples of the Sea, and the same marauders apparently had a hand in destroying the Hittite Empire in Asia Minor. Then Troy fell and the powerful civilization of Mycenae was wiped out by barbarians from the north. Throughout this period, waves of refugees from these upheavals lapped at the shores of all the lands that bordered on the Mediterranean.

Around 800 B.C. the Phoenicians were establishing themselves at Carthage in northern Africa. Mainland Greece was beginning to stir again, gathering its strength for the great burst of creative energy that was to become its Golden Age. Most of Italy, meanwhile, remained a tangle of agricultural and pastoral tribes—until the Etruscans appeared on the scene.

Where did they come from? Were they from abroad? Or were their ancestors native to Italy?

Underlying almost every Etruscan site are traces of earlier settlements. By 900 B.C. Italy—from Bologna in the north to a little south of Rome—had been lightly populated by Iron Age farmers who lived in small villages. They built round or rectangular huts of clay, reeds and wood; they were skilled metalworkers; they cremated their dead and buried the ashes in little clay containers shaped like their huts or in pottery urns that were covered with inverted bowls or helmet-shaped lids or actual helmets of bronze (page 20). They had no written language. Archeologists call the people of this culture Villanovans, from a site near Bologna where their remains were first identified by scholars more than a hundred years ago. In all probability, the Villanovans were the Etruscans' forebears.

The Villanovans represent but the first of many murky passages in the Etruscans' story, and not a few pages are altogether blank. Because Etruscan literature has vanished except for funerary and dedicatory inscriptions found mainly in tombs and temple ruins—and not all these writings are fully understood —the brief, radiant history of this people must be reconstructed from the contents of their tombs, from other physical evidence pieced together by archeologists and from Greek and Roman records.

Many of the Greek references written between 500 B.C. and the time of Christ that dealt with events beginning around 750 B.C. were unreliable. The legends tended to disparage the Tyrrhenoi as inferior and hostile. The early period, about which the Greeks wrote, was an era of vigorous competition—for trade, for minerals, for island and coastal bases, for sailing lanes at sea. Piracy became a fact of life among the sailors of Greece, Carthage and Etruria. The Romans,

In Tuscany the Etruscans chose dwelling places with a wary eye toward marauders, settling atop high natural ramparts; Volterra (right) was a typical hill town. Around 400 B.C. Volterra's residents were compelled to ring their city and its ancient cemetery with a fortifying wall. Erosion has since caused part of the town to plummet into the ravine beneath, exposing graves that appear here as tiny holes in the cliffside. A stretch of the old Etruscan wall can be seen below the abandoned Christian monastery that now dominates the site.

too, when they had grown powerful enough to subdue the Etruscans after the Fourth Century B.C., put their own interpretation on history. Yet by the accounts of both, Etruria from its earliest days was a force to be feared and envied.

According to the Greeks, the Etruscans were a supreme seafaring power—and also an affliction. The geographer-historian Strabo, writing at the dawn of Christianity, reported that "men were so afraid of the pirate vessels of the Tyrrhenians and the savagery of the barbarians in this region that they would not so much as sail there for trading."

They were as dangerous on land as they were at sea. Their military success in Italy itself may be attributed to armaments and battle techniques adopted from the Greeks. For example, their infantry used a phalanx formation similar to that of the Greek army —a closely massed body of advancing men spurred to greater effort by the blaring of bronze war trumpets. These infantrymen went into battle with a secret weapon: sturdy shoes of leather that laced firmly about the ankle. If the truth were known, shoes may have won more battles for the Etruscans than did weapons or arms.

The story of Etruscan expansion concerns itself as much with material and industrial growth, however, as it does with conquest of territory. As Etruria acquired strength, her cities became specialists in crafts or products. Fufluna for instance—later called Populonia by the Romans—became the center of the iron industry. Tarquinii grew rich from its exports of bronze utensils. Pottery and metalwork were the principal output of Caere. And nowhere were there sculptors whose work equaled that of Veii's artisans. The rise of such centers overlapped one another in

Text continued on page 16

Crossroads of Culture and Trade

The boundaries of Etruria (large map at right) changed with the military and economic fortunes of its people. Over the nearly six centuries of the Etruscans' history, however, their wealthiest and most populous centers constituted a territory of about 15,000 square miles in north-central Italy. It contained about a dozen cities and was roughly bounded by the Arno River to the north, the Tiber River to the south and east, and the Tyrrhenian Sea on the west. Though the Etruscans ventured on land as far north as the Po Valley and as far south as the Bay of Naples, their contacts with the rest of the ancient world were based on overseas trade: exporting metals and farm produce and bringing home products ranging from olive oil to gold.

The gradual Roman takeover of Etruria, after the Fourth Century B.C., brought about the renaming of its cities in Latin. As a result many of the original Etruscan names, which were rooted in a language that scholars have yet to unlock, were lost completely. The first column of the glossary at right lists the Etruscan place names that have survived. For some, identification or spelling is incomplete (indicated by dashes or parenthetical letters); for others, spellings are purely speculative (indicated by a question mark). The glossary's center column provides the Latin versions of known Etruscan towns. The third column lists the modern names of all the sites mentioned in this volume.

Etruria's central location (square in the map below) made it a focal point for the bustling Mediterranean world. Functioning as a kind of sophisticated clearing house for Eastern developments ranging from the arts to technology, Etruria synthesized such ideas and handed them to the Romans, who used the bequest to build first a city—and then an empire.

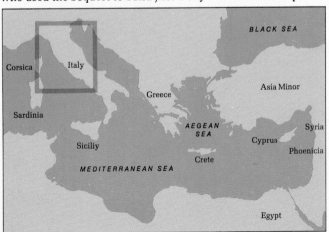

ETRUSCAN	LATIN	MODERN
	Arretium	Arezzo
Felsina	Bononia	Bologna
Velsna, Velzna	Volsinii	Bolsena
Capeva	Capua	Capua
	Castellum Axium	Castel d'Asso
Cisra	Caere	Cerveteri
Ceisna (?)	Caesena	Cesena
Clevsin	Clusium	Chiusi
	Falerii Veteres	Civita Castellana
	Spina	Comacchio
Curtun-	Cortona	Cortona
Vi(p)sul-	Faesulae	Fiesole
	Florentia	Florence
	Pithecusae	Ischia
Manuva	Mantua	Mantua
Mutina	Mutina	Modena
Cusa	Cosa	Orbetello
	Urbs Vetus	Orvieto
Per(u)sna	Perusia	Perugia
	Placentia	Piacenza
	Pompeii	Pompeii
Fufluna	Populonia	Populonia
	Graviscae	Porto Clementino
Rav(e)na	Ravenna	Ravenna
Arimna (?)	Ariminum	Rimini
Ruma (?)	Roma	Rome
	Rusellae	Roselle
	Punicum	Santa Marinella
	Pyrgi	Santa Severa
Saena (?)	Saena	Siena
Sveama-	Suana	Sovana
Sudri, Suthri	Sutrium	Sutri
Tarchna	Tarquinii	Tarquinia
Veia	Veii	Veio
Vetluna	Vetulonia	Vetulonia
Surina (?)	Sorrina	Viterbo
Velauri	Volaterrae	Volterra
Velc, Velecha (?)	Vulci	Vulci

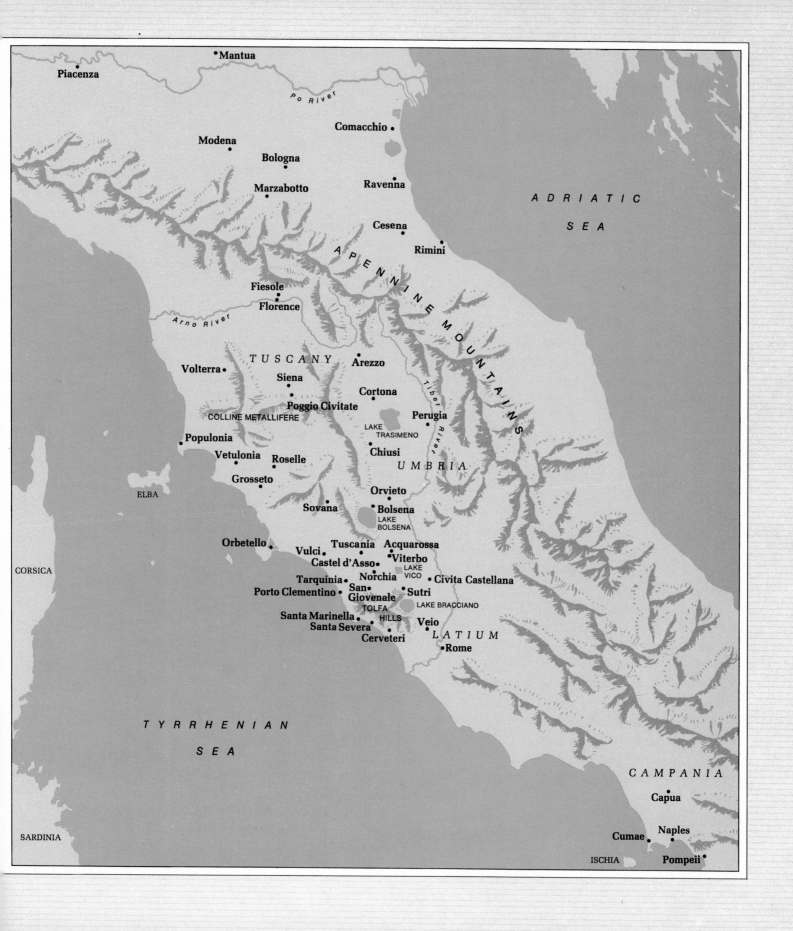

time; as one reached the peak of its productivity, another would come into its own.

It all began, though, with metal. Throughout the Etruscans' tenure, their base of strength was control of the mineral resources in the area from the Tolfa Hills, just west of Lake Bracciano, to the famed Colline Metallifere—the metal-bearing hills of Tuscany. From ore deposits in these regions came an abundance of copper, lead, iron and tin.

But early in the Sixth Century B.C., the Etruscans were also taking iron from the island of Elba, where the ore lay near the surface in supplies so vast that the Etruscans believed the mines filled up again, by magic, as fast as the metal was removed.

For many years the Etruscans smelted Elba's ore right on the spot. But eventually they established a mainland processing plant at Fufluna. Already a prosperous Etruscan bronze-producing center near the site of modern Piombino, Fufluna faced iron-rich Elba across a six-mile-wide strait.

By 400 B.C. Fufluna had grown into a great industrial city, the Pittsburgh or Essen of its time, and the only major city the Etruscans ever developed directly on the seashore, a location that in most circumstances was regarded as too vulnerable to attack. In its heyday Fufluna consisted of two zones. On the sea was the industrial sector with its iron furnaces, forges and foundries, its ore port and its naval arsenal. In the city's upper zone, perched on a high promontory and well separated from the industrial area with its belching smoke and smelly fish, were the homes and temples, and also a tower from which fishermen watched for schools of tuna. Residents of upper Fufluna commanded a view of a harbor busy with merchantmen and the great iron-ore barges, plying back and forth across the six miles of water separating their promontory from Elba.

Sunset fell on processions of weary men walking upward toward home: metalworkers stained from the grime and smoke of their furnaces and forges, bargemen encrusted with ore dust and salt spray.

Along Fufluna's docks rose enormous piles of crude iron and finished wares for export, and tons of ore yet to be smelted—mined not only on Elba but at nearby mainland sites. How much iron was extracted from the ore delivered to Fufluna nobody will ever know for sure. Mountains of slag—the waste product of the furnaces—accumulated in the neighborhood of the city; but since World War I, when iron became scarce in Italy, these heaps have been mined by local workers for the metal they still contain. Experts have estimated that the weight of the original slag heaps was more than two million tons, indicating that the Etruscans of Fufluna and its vicinity must have extracted and worked from 10,000 to 12,000 tons of iron ore every year for 400 years.

What iron was for Fufluna, bronze was for Tarquinii. Situated five miles from the sea on a ridge about 40 miles north of Rome, Tarquinii reached the pinnacle of its economic power early in the Seventh Century B.C., when it became the richest and most influential of all Etruscan cities. Until about 650 B.C., Tarquinii—whose metalworkers were the finest artisans on the Italian peninsula—dominated its world. Bronze weaponry, candelabra and other household goods, figurines and elaborately decorated cauldrons poured out of its workshops for the Tarquinians' own use and for their domestic and overseas trade.

By 650 B.C. economic leadership had passed to the city of Caere, slightly south of Tarquinii. Here, near the copper, iron and lead mines of the Tolfa Hills, Caere's craftsmen caught up with and surpassed those of Tarquinii and in addition developed a flourishing trade in goldwork and an especially fine variety of *bucchero*—the distinctive black Etruscan pottery with a deliberately metallic sheen *(page 63)*.

By the beginning of the Sixth Century B.C. the city of Vulci, north of Tarquinii, had risen to prominence as a major artistic center. Vulci was noted for its sculptures in bronze and stone, but the finest sculptors of early Etruria were to appear in Veii, 12 miles north of Rome. By the end of the Sixth Century B.C., Veii had a flourishing school of terra-cotta sculpture and a master sculptor, Vulca, the only Etruscan artist whose name has survived the centuries. It probably was Vulca who made the famous Apollo of Veii *(page 103)*. So celebrated was Vulca that he was called to Rome, which by his day had burgeoned into a city, to make a statue of Jupiter for the great temple erected on the Capitoline Hill.

Emboldened by the ease with which their warriors could roll over any local opposition, and enriched by natural resources, skills and trade, the Etruscans moved outward in all directions from their rich base in central Italy. By 600 B.C. they dominated all the western shore of the peninsula, from Pisa to Rome, and had crossed the Tiber River to control much of the present province of Campania.

Eventually they established a powerful city on the Volturno River at the site of Capua near Naples and controlled parts of the south all the way to the modern city of Salerno. But around Naples, they collided with the powerful Greek colony of Cumae, whose residents refused to be dislodged by the pioneers from the north. Ultimately, the Greeks were able, by force, to reverse the Etruscans' southward thrust.

The final Etruscan push, then, was northeastward from their central base. About 550 B.C. they managed to cross the great barrier of the Apennine ridge, to colonize in the flat, fertile region of the Po River valley and to set up a chain of towns along the Adriatic south of modern Venice. Only the bellicose Venetian tribes in the extreme northeast held firm against the Etruscans. Nonetheless, from their coastal cities the Etruscans were able to command the Adriatic, as they did the Tyrrhenian.

Fortunately for students of history and humanity, as the Etruscans grew increasingly powerful and wealthy, into the tombs of their mighty went the accumulating treasures of Etruria, as well as household goods and weapons for personal use in eternity. It is from the detailed wall paintings and the abundant accouterments in their graves that we have learned most of what we know about this civilization. The acres and acres of cemeteries around their cities provide a vivid picture of the Etruscans as they were in life—not only as city builders, warriors and traders, but also as appealing, vivacious people with exquisite taste and a passion for the good life.

One of the richest of these finds, the contents of which make up the core of the Vatican's Gregorian Etruscan Museum, is the so-called Regolini-Galassi Tomb near the ruins of Caere *(pages 47-55)*. It dates from around 650 B.C. and takes its present name from the unlikely partnership of a priest and a military man —Father Alessandro Regolini and Generàl Vincenzo Galassi—who, drawn together by a common enthusiasm for archeology, excavated it in 1836.

The tomb was one of a half dozen that lay beneath the remains of a great earthen mound encircled by two tufa walls, the outer one more than 50 yards in diameter. Five of the tombs, on the periphery of the mound and of a later date, had been sacked before Father Regolini and General Galassi arrived to explore the most ancient center section. There they discovered an unplundered tomb, entered through a long sloping dromos, or walkway, beyond which was the main chamber, a corridor-like space about 24 feet long and four feet wide. The lower part of both the dromos and this main chamber had been hacked out of the living tufa, and the upper walls built up of large square tufa blocks laid in tiers that inclined inward to form an enclosed vault. Near the entrance of the main chamber two oval compartments, cut into the bedrock, opened to the left and right.

Along the dromos, the excavators came upon the first of three burials: the powdered bones of a warrior lying upon a bronze couch. Beside the couch was a four-wheeled bronze funeral wagon. An iron sword and 10 bronze javelins rested near him, and eight round bronze shields (obviously ornamental since they were too flimsy to have been used in combat) were nailed to a wall of the dromos. The warrior's other grave goods—which overflowed into another compartment—included bronze cauldrons, andirons of bronze and iron, a wheeled bronze incense burner and bronze disks decorated with griffins.

The compartment to the right contained only one item: a great fluted pottery urn with a domed lid topped by the headless figurine of a horse. It held the ashes of a man—probably a relative of the noble personages buried nearby.

But the most astonishing finds lay in the main chamber and belonged to an Etruscan noblewoman. Inscribed on the table service of silver cups and bowls was the name Larth, perhaps the woman's husband. Scattered around the crumbled bones, crushed by masonry fallen from the roof, was a treasure in wrought gold. The most spectacular piece was a great gold fibula, or pin, more than a foot high (page 55). Other items included a massive gold ornament like a breastplate, long gold earrings, armlets and necklaces. The woman's remains lay amid a heap of little gold plaques that once must have formed an entire garment, sewn onto some supporting fabric long since rotted away. And close at hand, for gaming in the next world, were five pairs of ivory dice.

Besides confirming that the Etruscans were enormously prosperous, the contents of the Regolini-Galassi Tomb provide proof that Etruria was strongly influenced from its beginnings by the cultures in the eastern Mediterranean. Materials that had to be imported via Near Eastern trade—ivory, gold, amber—were in the find. And many locally made objects had a distinctly Near Eastern flavor, their motifs showing influences from Egypt, Mesopotamia and the Levant. Indeed, objects of eastern and Greek manufacture occur in some of the earliest Etruscan burials, dating from 750 to 700 B.C.

But apparently nothing aroused greater Etruscan delight than the works of Greeks or Greek-trained artisans. The Etruscans remained so smitten by the arts of Greece that tombs dating from their wealthiest period, between 600 and 400 B.C., have yielded more Greek vases than has all Greece itself.

Further stunning evidence of Etruria's artistic preference came to light in 1969 and 1970, during an excavation near the site of Tarquinii. The dig, led by

Text continued on page 22

Early Dwellers on the Land

The people known as Villanovans—the name derives from a rich archeological site near modern Bologna—were the immediate predecessors of the Etruscans in the land that became Etruria. It cannot flatly be said that the Villanovans were the Etruscans' ancestors; as yet, scholars know too little about the Etruscans' lineage. Nevertheless, the Villanovans provided the underpinnings for Etruscan civilization, which would perpetuate and refine many of their skills, customs and beliefs.

By the Eighth Century B.C., clusters of Villanovan hut settlements existed throughout central Italy. Although primarily farmers, the inhabitants were highly skilled in pottery making and metalwork; they created some of their finest wares to hold the cremated remains of their dead—as the Etruscans would later also do (pages 89-91). From the insights provided by such grave goods, archeologists can reconstruct significant elements of the Villanovans' way of life.

Shaped like a circular hut, an Eighth Century B.C. terra-cotta cinerary urn is a replica of the deceased's home. The object, 13 inches high, provides details of the Villanovan house: interlocking roof timbers, an opening over the door to allow smoke to escape, the round roof bordered with a repetitive motif, and the door and walls gaily decorated with abstract designs.

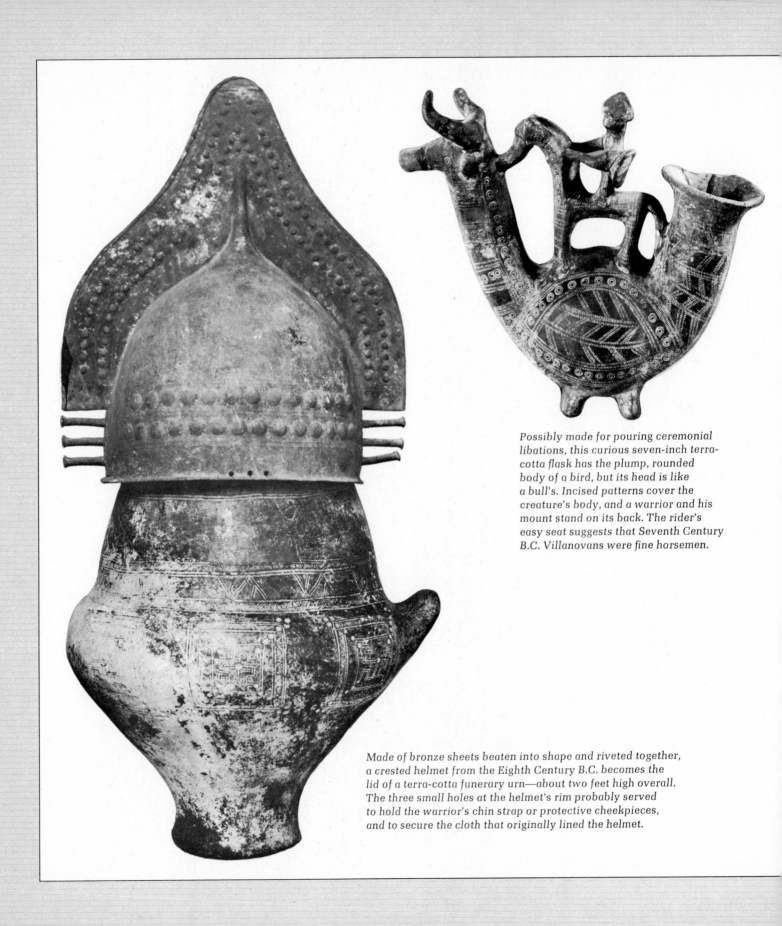

Possibly made for pouring ceremonial
libations, this curious seven-inch terra-
cotta flask has the plump, rounded
body of a bird, but its head is like
a bull's. Incised patterns cover the
creature's body, and a warrior and his
mount stand on its back. The rider's
easy seat suggests that Seventh Century
B.C. Villanovans were fine horsemen.

Made of bronze sheets beaten into shape and riveted together,
a crested helmet from the Eighth Century B.C. becomes the
lid of a terra-cotta funerary urn—about two feet high overall.
The three small holes at the helmet's rim probably served
to hold the warrior's chin strap or protective cheekpieces,
and to secure the cloth that originally lined the helmet.

Two concentric circles of tiny figures adorn the lid and shoulder of this 12-inch bronze vessel from the Eighth Century B.C. Foreshadowing the prebattle dancing that was to become an Etruscan custom, the Villanovan images apparently are moving in tempo around a chained animal—either a monkey or a bear—in a propitiatory ceremony before a hunt. One man prods a long-horned bullock. Others carry weapons, or are beating their shields as though they were cymbals.

the Italian archeologist Mario Torelli, was initiated primarily to probe the Roman port of Graviscae near the mouth of the Marta River. The excavators explored the Roman works as they had planned, but in the process they found—partly underneath the Roman site and partly adjacent to it—an extensive Etruscan port.

What surprised the archeologists most, however, was hard evidence that a colony of Greek merchants had lived in the port, side by side with the Etruscans, from around 580 B.C. In one corner of the town were the remains of a Greek temple and a sacred area dedicated to the Greek goddesses Hera, Demeter and Aphrodite. More than 1,500 votive oil lamps—all imported from Greece, all blackened from use—were dug from these ruins. So were many beautiful Greek vases, some bearing Greek inscriptions.

The most exciting discovery was an inscribed stone about four and a half feet high, originally part of a pyramidal funerary monument. It represented the Greek god Apollo and bore a message: "I belong to Apollo of Aegina. Sostratos had me made." The reference fits startlingly into the corpus of written history: the Greek historian Herodotus, in the Fifth Century B.C., mentioned an earlier Greek named Sostratos, of the island of Aegina, whom he described as one of the most successful merchants of all time, a man whose commercial interests ranged from Aegina itself to lands as distant as Spain.

But the Greeks were not the only great seafarers who figured prominently in Etruscan life. Classical records testify that the Etruscans also had ties with another great maritime power: Carthage, in northern Africa. The bond between these peoples lacked the esthetic element—especially the shared love of fine artworks—that characterized the Etruscans' affinity with the Greeks. In dealings with Carthage, whose people deserved to be noted more as businessmen and fighters than as artists, the relationship was strictly practical. Herodotus wrote of an alliance between the two powers; and Aristotle, who pondered the juxtaposition of commercial ties and mutual protection treaties in his *Politics,* cited the bond between the Tyrrhenians and the Carthaginians as a prime example of such a political arrangement.

The tie was tightened by the presence of an enemy whom both the Etruscans and the Carthaginians wanted out of the way. Ironically, the nuisance was a band of Greeks—actually, colonists based on the island of Corsica, from which they launched naval raids to intercept Etruscan and Carthaginian merchant ships. Sometime around 535 B.C. fleets from the city of Caere joined forces with Carthaginian sailors and battled the Greeks off Corsica. A severe blow was dealt the bothersome Greeks, and Corsica was wrested from them. The Etruscans gained control of the island and the Carthaginians, by mutual agreement, became lords over adjacent Sardinia.

Corroboration of the bond between Etruria and Carthage came to light in 1964 at Pyrgi, a shipping port for the city of Caere. Within the confines of the sanctuary, archeologists found three thin gold sheets (*page 41*) folded up like letters ready to be put into envelopes. Two were inscribed in the Etruscan language, and one in Phoenician, a Carthaginian tongue. Written around 500 B.C., their similar texts recorded the dedication by the ruler of Caere of a shrine to a goddess whom the Carthaginians worshipped as Astarte and the Etruscans as Uni. The fact that the sheets carry the same message in both languages establishes the presence at Pyrgi of at least a small colony of Carthaginians; both tongues had to be used so that all inhabitants could understand.

Sometime after 500 B.C. the gold sheets had been wrenched from their original mounts on the sanctuary walls, folded up and buried, presumably to hide them from some plundering enemy force. Twenty-nine of the little gold-headed nails that once held them in place were found carefully placed within the folds. It was because of this hasty burial that the precious documents miraculously managed to survive.

Among the mysteries that bedevil scholars is the question of how the Etruscans got to the sea from their inland sites. Their only major city right on the sea was the great metal-producing center of Fufluna. Up and down the long Tyrrhenian shoreline, from which they sailed with such success, there is today only one anchorage that a modern sailor would find secure—a protected bay about halfway between ancient Fufluna and Tarquinii. Everywhere else on the coast treacherous winds whip everything under sail. The sea crashes onto submerged barriers and long sandbanks, and in inclement weather the homebound sailor reluctantly puts back out to avoid certain disaster. Surely, it would seem, Etruscan vessels must have been forced to do the same.

Moreover, in Roman times great stretches of the seacoast, from Caere to Tarquinii and farther north, were swampy and considered unhealthy because of what the Romans called gravis aer, the bad air. The term implies that malaria may have been a common affliction. Certainly, from the time of Christ through the Renaissance, the region was uninhabitable because of that scourge. How did the Etruscans manage to live there—or sail from there?

From aerial surveys and sophisticated underwater archeological studies now underway (pages 147-153), the answer appears to be that the geography of the Tyrrhenian coast has undergone considerable change since Etruscan days. Then, at or near the mouths of rivers, there existed large natural lagoons, some of them joined to the sea by channels through which the Etruscans' shallow-draft ships could easily maneuver. At some point before Roman times, when the Etruscans were in decline, the entrances and exits to the lagoons were allowed to silt up with soil washed down from hills, which by then had been denuded of forests, and the lagoons themselves turned into swamps. They remained so until vast drainage projects in the 20th Century transformed them—not into lagoons again, but into arable land.

In ancient times men were helpless against land changes wrought by the sea. But the Etruscans were amazingly successful in contending with the elements inland; they were skilled as hydraulic engineers. They learned to cope with the twin problems of erosion and flooding, which were especially serious in the sharply scarped landscape of southern Etruria. The very streams that carved out the tufa plateaus on which their cities stood had to be prevented from eating away the Etruscans' roads and inundating their fields. Their solution was to dig an intricate series of underground passages, called cuniculi by the Romans (pages 128, 129). These conduits served to channel and direct surface water. They were tall enough for a man to stand in, about half a yard wide, and had frequent shaftlike openings to the surface that provided access for Etruscan workmen. Having caught and captured the waters of flooding streams, the cuniculi then carried them away from areas that otherwise would have been waterlogged and made useless. The process created fields for cultivation where none had existed before. More than 28 miles of cuniculi have been traced at Etruscan sites northwest of Rome, 15 miles of them in and around Veii alone.

In the vicinity of Veii, another notable achievement of Etruscan engineering is an efficient network of all-weather roads hacked out of the tufa. At Vulci, the Etruscans applied their ingenuity to bridge building. There is a high, vaulting span over the fuming little Fiora River; the Romans constructed this bridge upon sturdy Etruscan foundations.

All these engineering skills were eventually bestowed upon budding little Rome, which burst into full bloom under a series of Etruscan rulers. Within a hundred years after the first of them mounted the Roman throne late in the Seventh Century B.C., the Etruscans had modeled an amorphous collection of settlements along the Tiber into a true city. Where they found huts, they left temples. They drained the swampy area that was to become the site of the Roman Forum. They laid the foundations of the city's first sewer system—whose central channel, the Cloaca Maxima, is still visible today.

In addition they introduced to Rome a Greek surveying instrument (page 125), known in Latin as the groma. This device was to prove invaluable to the men who were to become the ancient world's most famous engineers and town planners.

Rome's history, around its traditional founding date of 753 B.C., is shrouded in a mist of myth. The figures of Romulus and Remus, twin sons—sired, so their mother said, by the god Mars—dominate this fog most dramatically. Condemned to death by a jealous ruler who was their mother's uncle, so the legend goes, the twins were left to perish on the banks of the Tiber River, where they were discovered by a friendly female wolf who nursed them until a shepherd picked them up and took them home to his wife. When the twins grew up, each with his own supporters fought for the prerogatives of establishing the city; Remus was killed by his brother's faction, and Romulus became Rome's founding father.

Once that yarn and more tales about successive generations of rulers and heroes are out of the way, however, an Etruscan stands as Rome's first historical character. The Romans called him Lucius Tarquinius—his original name has been lost—and he was the son of a wealthy Corinthian Greek refugee, Demaratus. He probably began life as a resident of the Etruscan city of Tarquinii, where he married a formidable Etruscan noblewoman named Tanaquil. As Livy told it, Tarquinius moved to Rome, became its king in 616 B.C. and founded the Tarquin Dynasty, which was to last more than a century.

How this foreigner actually achieved the throne is not clear. In his history of Rome, Livy said that he made friends with the reigning king, that he was free both with his money and with "a kindly word." He was, wrote Livy, "the first to canvass personally for votes, and to have delivered a public speech designed to win popular support." He may have found knots of Etruscan merchants and fellow immigrants already in Rome willing to support him.

It is equally possible that Tarquinius took the throne by force. Perhaps he was a soldier of fortune with an army of his own; it is fairly certain that such

A Third Century B.C. bronze coin that was minted at Fufluna commemorates the town's vigorous smelting industry, symbolized by a hammer and tongs. The four pellets stamped between the tools indicated the coin's value. Fufluna became a metal-processing center in the Seventh Century B.C., first with copper and bronze, and later with iron. By the time this coin was struck, Fufluna was Etruria's smelting capital.

bands existed in Etruscan times, lending their services to various cities for a fee. It is possible that for some reason he had been called to Rome with his mercenary army; and once there, his martial business accomplished, he decided to stay.

Tarquinius was succeeded by his son-in-law, Servius Tullius—also, in all likelihood, an Etruscan; it may have been face-saving Roman writers who converted him—as someone did—into a "Latin" (page 27). Servius' successor was Tarquinius Superbus —given the latter name because of his arrogance. The dynasty ended, according to traditional history, when Superbus' lecherous and tyrannical son Sextus raped a virtuous Roman lady named Lucretia and she killed herself to expunge the disgrace. Superbus had long been hated for his tyrannical ways, and this final out-

rage triggered a revolt that cast the Tarquins from Rome in 509 B.C. and inflamed the ensuing hostility between Romans and Etruscans.

So goes heroic Roman tradition. Embattled heroes on both sides dominate its next phase: the Roman soldier Horatius and his Etruscan counterpart, Lars Porsenna. The story of their violent encounter has survived more than two millennia, strengthened along the way by Thomas Babington Macaulay's stirring and romantic *Lays of Ancient Rome*. His was the famous passage about Horatius confronting the army of Lars Porsenna at the bridge:

Hew down the bridge, Sir Consul,
With all the speed ye may;
I, with two more to help me,
Will hold the foe in play.

The narrative actually involved Rome against the Etruscans—though not many English-speaking school children were aware of it while memorizing Macaulay's 19th Century tum-te-tum verses. Lars Porsenna, who launched the attack on Rome, was ruler of the Etruscan city of Clusium—Chiusi on a modern map. Battle was joined on the first bridge that spanned the Tiber—the Pons Sublicius, a wooden structure, which could indeed be hewn down. Horatius, so the story goes, held out on the far side of the bridge while his companions hewed. When the bridge finally fell, Horatius dived into the Tiber and swam back to the Roman shore, armor and all.

According to Livy, Lars Porsenna then besieged Rome, but was so impressed by the courage of its defenders that he sued for peace. Other Roman historians, Tacitus among them, contradict Livy and say that Lars Porsenna took Rome. Modern scholars attest that this is in fact what happened; Lars Porsenna's victory made him one more in the line of Etruscan rulers with sufficient strength to impose their power on the city.

However, the Etruscans' hold on Rome ended once and for all in 506 B.C., when Etruscan forces led by Lars Porsenna's son were routed at Aricia, just south of Rome, by Latin soldiers aided by Greeks.

For however long they ruled Rome, the Etruscans' legacy extended into art, architecture, custom, dress, social and military organization—and religion: they bequeathed the religio-civic use of augurs to foretell auspicious conditions for everything from city founding to wars, for great ventures of all kinds.

From the Etruscans too came the trappings of temporal authority: the *sella curulis*: a folding chair with curved legs and no back that became the magistrates' chair, and the fasces, a bundle of rods bound around a central ax that symbolized the rulers' power to flog or execute. (The latter became an all-too-familiar emblem in the 20th Century when Mussolini adopted it as his party's own.) Another Etruscan bequest was the "triumph"; in its Roman form, it was a ceremony in which a victorious general rode into the city in splendor, standing in a chariot at the head of a procession of soldiers and prisoners, on his way to make grateful sacrifice to the gods on the Capitoline Hill.

Perhaps most important, Etruscans created for Rome the persistent glory of the Capitoline Hill itself. Until the Tarquins ruled Rome, no one considered this little hill important. But Etruscan kings chose it and erected upon it a great temple to the citizens' prime deity, Jupiter, whom the Etruscans equated with their own god Tinia; the sanctuary also honored the Roman goddesses Juno and Minerva, whose Etruscan equivalents were Uni and Menrva.

Thus this modest hillock became the religious and political heart of the Roman republic and later of the empire. Two and a half millennia later, the Capitoline—now the Campidoglio—is still the center of Rome's municipal government. It was to the Campidoglio that the foreign ministers of Europe went in March 1957 to sign the agreements that created the Common Market—the first tentative attempt at European unification since the 200-year period of the Pax Romana, which ended in 180 A.D.

But today, Rome is not the place where memory of Etruria's greatness is most vivid. It is farther north, in the region of Tuscany, where the Etruscans' presence can still be sensed most acutely.

Could it be coincidence, could it be simply something in the air or in the water? Somehow there are traces of Etruscan speech patterns still discernible today in the Italian dialect spoken in Tuscany—the aspirate sound of the Tuscan "c," which is pronounced as if it were "h." Is it a folk memory, a strain still of Etruscan blood, or one of history's jokes: the enigmatic smile on the lips of Etruscans in tomb paintings, or quirked on the faces of men and women on sarcophagus lids, lingering like the smile of the Cheshire cat long after the cat has disappeared?

The English writer D. H. Lawrence, when he visited the tombs and museums of Etruria early in the 20th Century, did not put it in these terms, but he too saw the Etruscans' illusory image in Italy: "How much more Etruscan than Roman the Italian of today is: sensitive, diffident, craving really for symbols and mysteries, able to be delighted with true delight over small things, violent in spasms, and altogether without sternness or natural will-to-power."

In Tribute to the Heroes from Vulci

Chauvinist Roman chroniclers played down the fact that a number of their kings were of Etruscan origin. A case in point is Servius Tullius, ruler of Rome during the Sixth Century B.C. In Latin accounts, Servius may have been either a Roman slave's child or the son of a captured noblewoman —in any case not Etruscan-born.

Servius' origin in Etruria was not confirmed until 1857, when Alessandro François, a Florentine of French extraction, discovered wall paintings in a tomb at Vulci. The figures in the frescoes and the identifications beside them—added to scraps of information from other sources—established Servius Tullius as a man from Vulci; he was originally named Mastarna.

The paintings in the so-called François Tomb were commissioned around the Third Century B.C., most likely by the wealthy Etruscan at right. The date coincides roughly with the time when Vulci succumbed to Rome. In that context, the paintings can be viewed as calculated reminders of a triumphant time when Etruscans occupied the throne of Rome.

In this earliest full-length portrait of an Etruscan, an anonymous painter memorialized his benefactor, who is attended by a dwarf servant holding a hunting hawk. The patron, named Vel Saties, had the same artist do the sequence from Etruscan history reproduced on the following pages.

Caelius Vibenna (left) holds up his bound hands so that
Mastarna can unbind them with a sword cut; an empty sheath
and another sword—probably to rearm Caelius—are under
Mastarna's left arm. This painting was divided vertically
when all the frescoes were removed to Rome in 1862.

Bold Rescue and Swift Vengeance

The historian Livy's version of Servius Tullius' rise to the Roman kingship *(page 68)*—in which a boy of doubtful parentage, who was adopted by a scheming queen, is marked for greatness by supernatural portents —has all the earmarks of pure myth. In straightforward context are the François Tomb paintings: depictions of combat between the men of Vulci and their enemies. When combined with references in Classical literature and supplementary findings by archeologists, the paintings tell a convincing story of conquest by a people at the height of their power.

The frescoes' scenes are set in the Sixth Century B.C., 300 years earlier than the wall paintings were commissioned. At that time, forces led by Mastarna of Vulci, allied with those of two local brothers, Caelius and Aulus Vibenna, fought a coalition that included several other Etruscan cities and Rome. When the Romans captured Caelius, Mastarna and Aulus rushed to the rescue. Later Mastarna, his name changed to Servius Tullius, took over the throne of Rome and reigned—according to the First Century A.D. historian-Emperor Claudius —"to the great good of the state."

Holding his vanquished enemy by the hair, a soldier of Vulci finishes off a Roman officer whose name identifies him as a member of the royal family. Some time after his triumph in battle, Mastarna went to Rome, assumed a new name and became king; whether he did so immediately to seal his conquest, or whether in fact there were subsequent lengthy political maneuverings, is a matter of dispute.

In this vividly reconstructed melee, three brave men from Vulci triumphantly stab their foes. Near the head of each man, victor and vanquished, is written his name, as well as the home city of each victim. The latter include the Etruscan cities of Volsinii, Suana and Falerii Veteres, thus confirming that Vulci was at war with a coalition of those cities as well as with Rome and so had good reason to be proud. The man at far right is identified as Aulus Vibenna, Caelius' brother.

To the ancients who wrote of the Etruscans, there was always something alien and strange about them. And as for modern writers, even the most admiring are forced, eventually, to use the word "mysterious" or its more elegant near-synonym "enigmatic."

The enigma lies in two closely related problems. First, what were the origins of the Etruscans: Were they newcomers to Italy, driven from a home somewhere else, or were they of indigenous Italic stock, just a sophisticated new generation sprung from cruder, more primitive forebears? And the second unanswered query, one that if resolved would shed bright light on the first, is: What was their language? The search for answers leads through a tangled web of conflicting evidence—literary, archeological, linguistic and plain circumstantial.

In the Etruscans' own time the Greek historian Herodotus, writing in the Fifth Century B.C., settled the matter of origin—once, and almost for all. Looking back some eight centuries, Herodotus said that the Etruscans had come from Lydia, an ancient nation in west-central Asia Minor. His direct, unequivocal account was this:

"A great famine is said to have occurred in the whole of Lydia. For some time the Lydians persisted in carrying on their usual life. But as the evil, instead of subsiding, continued to grow in violence, the king divided the Lydian people into two groups; and he drew lots for one of them to stay, the other to leave. Those Lydians who were designated by lot to leave the country went down to Smyrna, built ships, loaded these ships with all their household effects, and set sail to seek a territory until, after skirting the shores of many lands, they reached the land of the Umbrians. There they founded towns, in which they live until this day."

Thus the historian left the immigrants on the west coast of Italy in the heart of Etruscan country. Because of his general reliability, and because he lived and wrote while Etruscans were just past the peak of their power, Herodotus' account of an Etruscan homeland in Asia Minor was accepted without question by most later Classical writers. The Roman philosopher Seneca obviously was in agreement when he noted that "Asia claims the Etruscans as its own"; and Strabo, Vergil, Horace, Plutarch and Cicero all tended to use the words Lydian and Etruscan interchangeably.

Herodotus had his way for more than 400 years. Then, shortly before the birth of Christ came another historian, Dionysius of Halicarnassus, with a conflicting theory. Dionysius, a Greek living in Rome, had an ax to grind. His age witnessed a sudden burst of history writing, most of it dedicated to enhancing the glory of Rome without too much regard for fact. The prevailing propagandists of the time traced Roman ancestry to Aeneas, the Trojan hero of Vergil's *Aeneid*. Dionysius, however, labored to prove that everything Roman, good and bad, originally came from Greece. But the cultural contribution of the Etruscans, who were so utterly different from everyone else in both language and custom, could not

This snarling Chimera—a fantastic beast with a lion's body, a snake for a tail and the head of a goat sprouting from its spine—was unearthed more than 400 years ago near Florence, where it had lain for almost 2,000 years. The discovery of the 30-inch-high bronze helped awaken scholars to the rich Etruscan past. Experts know that the inscription on its right foreleg refers to the Etruscans' chief god, Tinia, but much of the tongue of this shadowy people still cannot be understood.

possibly fit into Dionysius' historical construction. How, then, was their presence—and their strangeness—to be accounted for? Dionysius solved the problem by saying that the Etruscans had not migrated from anywhere; that they were autochthonous. In other words, they were an indigenous Italic people—barbarians (which in Dionysius' day meant not only non-Greek but also inferior).

Fully aware that his theory ran contrary to that of the Classical world's most honored historian, Dionysius buttressed his argument with personal observations about contemporary Lydians. He remarked that Etruscans "have not the same language as the Lydians, do not worship the same gods as the Lydians, do not have the same laws."

This stance left Herodotus and Dionysius facing each other across the centuries, the notions of each propounded by factions of passionate supporters summoning circumstantial evidence. Even today, long after Classical times, both schools of thought have their adherents.

Subscribers to the theory of migration from the East can cite as supporting evidence the Egyptian references to the notorious Peoples of the Sea. Hieroglyphic inscriptions mentioning these seafaring marauders list among them peoples who have been identified with some certainty as the Achaeans, the Lycians, the Philistines and the Sardinians. One group in the inventory is unfamiliar: the Teresh. Some scholars construe the name as a variant of Tyrsenoi, a Greek term for Etruscans.

Other circumstantial evidence suggesting that the Etruscans could have originated in or around Asia Minor is to be found—Dionysius to the contrary notwithstanding—in some of their own funerary architecture, as well as in certain social and religious practices. There is a haunting stylistic similarity between Etruscan rock-cut tombs in the vicinity of Lake Vico and some Lydian and Lycian tombs in Turkey; in both places, the burial chambers have façades resembling those of houses or temples. In discussing social customs, Herodotus observed that the Lydians and their cultural cousins the Lycians traced their lineage through both the male and female lines, as did the Etruscans. The Greeks, in contrast, plotted genealogy only through male ancestors. Herodotus also remarked that the women of Lydia and Lycia, like Etruscan women, were more privileged than the females of Greece and Rome. Moreover, the Etruscan art of soothsaying by reading the signs in animal livers (page 94) finds its nearest counterpart in the liver reading of the ancient Babylonians of Asia Minor.

Some of the strongest evidence for the "Eastern roots" theory comes from the physical remnants of Etruscan culture itself. Luxury items found in tombs from the Seventh Century B.C.—e.g., the Regolini-Galassi (pages 47-55), the Barberini and numerous others—are richly decorated with motifs familiar in Near Eastern art: lions, sphinxes, griffins; also palm trees and rosettes. There is little evidence that these motifs were used before about 700 B.C. Then, all at once, they appear throughout Etruria. These facts hint strongly at ties closer than those engendered by commercial contact; they argue for a bond of blood.

Then, too, there is the Etruscans' affinity for the sea, a fondness not shared by their predecessors on the peninsula—the Villanovans. This Etruscan bent could conceivably be construed as a folk memory of a migration across open water, as Herodotus said, or of a former existence as seafaring men of the East.

But the evidence for Dionysius' theory is also powerful. Except for Herodotus' report, there is no record whatever of a mass migration of half a Near Eastern nation nor of any other such huge shifting of people to the Italian peninsula at any point during the entire period between 1300 B.C.—the date at which Herodotus set the immigration of half of Lydia's populace to Italy—and 700 B.C., when influences from the East become clear in Etruscan remains. It is odd that a world that knew so well, and talked so much about, a relatively local upheaval such as the Trojan War would have paid no heed to a great invasion. The imposition of foreign power en masse on the tribes of Italy surely would not have gone unnoticed or unmentioned in the works of writers or bards.

Thus most modern scholars come to the conclusion that the truth must lie somewhere in the middle: probably the Etruscans had early roots in Italian soil, but it is impossible to ignore the clues that some ancestral Etruscans also came from abroad.

The riddle of the Etruscans is particularly exasperating because it need not have been. They are known to have produced a certain amount—perhaps an abundance—of written material; had enough survived, it might have put an end to long scholarly debate. Especially frustrating are the references by such Roman authors as Livy and Varro to Etruscan texts on religion and history. Apparently as early as the Sixth Century B.C., Roman schoolboys studied Etruscan literary works just as, later on, they did Greek and Latin ones. And as late as the First Century A.D. the Emperor Claudius, who had an Etruscan wife, wrote a 20-volume history of the people.

But all these books, and all the really intimate

knowledge that Rome had of Etruria, have disappeared. Perhaps the books, or Latin translations of them, perished in the sacking of Rome by Goths and Vandals in the Fifth Century A.D.; perhaps the last copies went in the piecemeal obliteration of the great international library at Alexandria, in Egypt—by Romans, by Byzantine Christians and finally by Arabs.

By the time the Roman Empire crumbled, in the Fourth Century A.D., the Etruscans had been fully absorbed into the Roman world. Their heartland, Etruria, made up the greater part of one of 11 Roman districts that the Emperor Augustus had organized in 27 B.C. Whatever Rome had acquired from the Etruscans—religious practices, engineering, artistry—had been so assimilated, so Romanized, that when Rome fell the very memory of the Etruscan presence fell with it. Only Rome had known Etruria by heart; and then Rome was no more.

Through the long night of the Middle Ages Etruscan houses crumbled, temples and town walls were pulled down by wretched peasants to provide construction materials for crude shelters or flimsy barricades against marauding warlords and invaders. Local strongmen moved onto the former Etruscan heights to mine their stones and to build directly over Etruscan foundations. Only the burial chambers remained, many of them discovered and inhabited by shepherds or wild animals; fragments of inscriptions and bits of bronze or iron or terra cotta were turned up by plowmen, and discarded.

So matters rested until the 15th Century A.D. when Europe emerged into the light of the Renaissance and scholars read again of Etruria in the writings of Greek and Roman historians.

Among the first to set about reviving the memory and burnishing the reputation of the Etruscans was a Dominican friar from the town of Viterbo. Friar Giovanni Nanni—or Annio of Viterbo, as he was also called—had all the instincts of an antiquarian. He loved old stones, eroded inscriptions, broken bits. He knew that Viterbo lay in the heart of Etruscan country and decided to prove the town's Etruscan origin and to chronicle its early history.

This was fine, except that as a historian the friar was a knave. In his zeal he invented documents and inscriptions, and then "translated" them as "lost works of antiquity" in a book first published in 1489. One of his fragments purported to be the edict of a king who decreed that "within one wall shall be included the three towns, Lungula, Vetulonia, and Tirsena, called Volturna, and the whole city thus formed shall be called Etruria or Viterbum." Moreover, he claimed that the Etruscan language was derived from Hebrew, on the assumption that the language of the Bible must be the oldest in the world and therefore the wellspring of all tongues.

Eventually, Annio of Viterbo was attacked by knowledgeable scholars as a charlatan and a forger of fragments. But the unscrupulous friar had accomplished one thing: he had resonantly revived the memory of the Etruscans.

Hardly more than 50 years later, three fabulous bronze statues were unearthed in Tuscany and were identified by Italian antiquarians as Etruscan. Although one of them—an exquisite figure of the goddess Minerva—has since been attributed to a Greek artisan, the other two are still counted as Etruscan masterpieces: the monstrous Chimera of the Fourth Century B.C. and the life-sized, toga-clad figure known as the Orator made during the Second

Century B.C. The Chimera was found near Arezzo, and the Orator near Perugia.

The Chimera is a figure from Greek mythology: a monster slain by the hero Bellerophon, whose mount was the great winged horse Pegasus. Etruscan artists were fond of monsters of all kinds and of this one in particular, re-creating it repeatedly with fanciful variations. Sometimes it was rendered with the head of a bull, a horse or a panther emerging from the creature's back or tail. The pose of the Arezzo Chimera—crouched and looking up as if facing an attacker—hints that it might once have formed part of a group including Bellerophon and his steed. The right foreleg bears the Etruscan word TINS'CVIL, which indicates that it was a gift or votive offering to Tinia, the Etruscans' chief deity. As found, the Chimera had lost part of both left legs, but its craftmanship was of such outstanding quality that the celebrated sculptor Benvenuto Cellini wrote of it in his notebooks and may even have had a hand in restoring it.

These fine bronzes—spectacular and certain evidence of the glories of Etruscan civilization—fired the imagination of scholars. Early in the 17th Century a Tuscan nobleman, Grand Duke Cosimo II, commissioned a study of Etruria in order to find out more about the vanished people who had once lived in his countryside.

A pugnacious Scottish schoolmaster named Thomas Dempster, who was then serving as professor of civil law at the University of Pisa, got the job. Dempster came from a long line of sword-swinging Scots known as much for their public irascibility as for their private scholarship. He was a precocious fellow—he claimed to have learned the alphabet in one hour at the age of three—and had become a university professor at the age of 17. Thereafter, Dempster had risen rapidly in scholarly reputation, despite the fact that brawling in the streets and quarreling with his peers forced him to change universities every two or three years. He also had his hands full with a young and beautiful wife whose honor had to be defended, repeatedly, by Dempster's sword.

At the Grand Duke's bidding Dempster devoted himself, between 1616 and 1625, to assiduous study of Etruscan artifacts in private collections, to literary references and to the language itself—which he, like Friar Nanni before him, tried to relate to Hebrew. His hard labor produced the monumental *Seven Books Concerning the Kingdom of Etruria*. For some reason this work remained unpublished for a century. When it finally appeared it sparked an interest in the Etruscans throughout Tuscany.

On December 29, 1726, 40 citizens of Cortona, joined by about 100 other Italian gentlemen fascinated by things Etruscan, formed the Etruscan Academy for the further study of the people and their archeological legacy. The annually elected head of the Cortona Academy was called *lucumo,* a Latinized version of the Etruscan title *lauchume*—meaning chief or king—a term known from Roman writings.

Members of the academy met twice a month for debates and the discussion of new finds. Their meetings were called Cortona Nights, and their somewhat Pickwickian proceedings were published in nine volumes between 1738 and 1795 under the sonorous title *Examples of Academic Dissertations Read Publicly in the Noble Etruscan Academy of the Most Ancient City of Cortona.* The academy still meets, though now sporadically, and the records of its long-ago discussions can be consulted in the library of the academy in the main square of modern Cortona.

Dempster's work also led to establishment of the world's first museum of Etruscan artifacts, the Archeological Museum of Volterra, founded in the middle of the 18th Century by a local prelate, Monsignor Mario Guarnacci.

By that time the enthusiasm for Etruscan remains was beginning to spread to Britain. In 1769, Josiah Wedgwood founded a ceramics factory in Staffordshire, England, and called it—and the town he built for the workers and his own family—Etruria. Around 1770 James Byres, a Scot who traveled in Italy, began to make detailed sketches of newly discovered tombs at Tarquinii. Three decades later England's Sir William Gell wrote the first book in English about Etruscan places, describing some of the hundreds of tombs that were being opened for the first time while he visited Tarquinii in 1828.

In Italy local landowners feverishly began to collect everything Etruscan they could find. Notable among these avid collectors was Napoleon Bonaparte's brother Lucien, who in 1814 had purchased from the Pope an entire principality, which contained many of the treasure-filled burial sites of the ancient Etruscan city of Vulci.

In the midst of these slapdash doings emerged one of Etruria's most earnest chroniclers: George Dennis. Born in England in 1814, Dennis was a self-taught Classicist who read Greek, Latin and six modern languages. In 1842 he set forth to explore the Etruscan world. For five years he tramped the length and breadth of the Etruscan homeland. Unlike Dempster, who had organized what was already known of the Etruscans, Dennis went in search of the not-yet-uncovered, the hidden. Fighting through underbrush, picking his way up and down precipitous cliffsides, hiring mules, quarreling with ill-informed guides and mendacious tomb plunderers, referring constantly to the existing Roman literary sources, Dennis finally produced the voluminous *Cities and Cemeteries of Etruria,* which was published in 1848.

He very nearly did for Etruria what blind Homer had done for Troy. Dennis was not a bard—though his subject did arouse poesy in him—and he did not engage himself much with heroes. Yet, more than a century after publication, his book is still required reading for anyone who wishes to learn about the Etruscans. Whoever reads Dennis carries forever after, in heart and mind, the shadows of the ancient people that still linger in the land of Etruria. Writing of an area near Viterbo, Dennis says:

"We were now on the great Etruscan plain, which was here and there darkened by woods. Tomb after tomb, hewn out of the cliffs, on either hand—a street of sepulchres; all with a strong house-like character. The solemnity of the site—the burial-place of long-past generations, of a people of mysterious origin and indefinite antiquity—their empty sepulchres yawning at our feet, yet their monuments still standing, in eternal memorial of their extinct civilization, and their epitaphs mocking their dust that has long ago been trampled under foot."

George Dennis' scholarly descendants, the Etruscologists of today, rarely give way to such romantic outbursts. Perhaps their sobriety is due to the impenetrable nature of the problem they face.

To begin with, no one yet knows what sort of language Etruscan was. If its roots were known, they might provide clues leading to a final resolution of that other persistent quandary about where the Etruscans originated. But like the second question, the one of language turns into a scholarly artichoke: as each leaf is carefully peeled away, it reveals another, which in turn discloses another. In the past, serious scholars—and numerous crackpots—have attempted to find the key to Etruscan in every known language in the world. So far nothing has worked.

One thing, however, has become apparent: Etruscan does not seem to belong to the Indo-European family of languages, the great group that includes most of the tongues of Europe, and of parts of the Near East and India. The Etruscan language's nearest possible relative exists on a stone grave marker on the island of Lemnos in the Greek archipelago. The monument, found by French archeologists in 1885, dates from the Sixth Century B.C. and the language of its inscription shows resemblances both to Etruscan and to the tongues of ancient Asia Minor. Although no actual relationship between the two languages has been proven, some scholars view the inscription on the Lemnos stele as a linguistic bridge linking the Etruscans to a Near Eastern homeland. But the evidence ends right there; no other bridge has turned up.

Some experts in ancient languages suggest that Etruscan was a tongue with Stone Age roots going back to a time long before Indo-European peoples settled in Italy—thus endorsing the presence there of a prehistoric non-Indo-European population.

Indeed, the uncertainty surrounding the Etruscan spoken language is so extreme that one commonly held impression is that the writing of the Etruscans is also undecipherable. But this is not true. It is not difficult for experts to "read" and pronounce the letters that make up the words. But since the language itself is almost entirely unknown, the words—apart from some names, dates, titles—convey no meaning.

The alphabet the Etruscans used is clear enough. It was derived from a form of Greek brought to Italy by colonists about 750 B.C.—probably the settlers of Ischia and Cumae. The Etruscan's borrowed alphabet consisted of 26 letters, but the number actually used varied from time to time and place to place. As the Etruscans adapted the imported alphabet to regional speech patterns, they found some sounds they did not need and others that had to be added or changed. Moreover, individual Etruscan cities altered the symbols they employed, presumably according

Random Remnants of a Lost Language

A scholar trying to decipher the Etruscan language is much like a starving man who is unable to find the key to a locked room richly stocked with food. Classicists know that Etruscan literature was extensive and that Roman schoolboys studied it both in the original language and in Latin translation. But a portion of only one book survives *(below)*—and it tells little.

Lacking full and varied texts, scholars attempting to compile a vocabulary have had to work with bits and pieces—words in religious and funerary inscriptions, and on mirrors and dice. Though some 10,000 inscriptions have turned up, studies of them have yielded few results. So far only 200 useful words have been identified.

Proper names inscribed beside known figures are among the few known Etruscan words. On the back of this seven-inch bronze mirror from the Third Century B.C., three identifiable goddesses—the Romans' Minerva (center), the scantily clad Venus and Juno (to Minerva's left)—were labeled Menrva, Turan and Uni.

A tiny portion of a mummy's linen wrapping, which bears the longest surviving text in Etruscan, refers to a sacred rite involving drinking and pouring of holy water. Scholars assume the body was that of an Etruscan woman who lived and died in Egypt.

Of the 59 words engraved on the stone scroll held by this life-sized effigy of a Third Century B.C. magistrate, most can be read. But they give little more than the man's genealogy and the names of various gods and cults.

Comparing two 2,500-year-old gold tablets—one in the known Phoenician tongue (top), the other in Etruscan —frustrated scholars who were trying to translate one from the other, since their texts are similar but not identical.

Study of the tablets above revealed one crucial bit of Etruscan: the word for "three," written as ci. It appeared on this pair of Etruscan dice from Tuscania, and is visible here on the farthest left face of the die at left.

to which of the Greek-speaking colonies they most commonly did business with.

In general, the Etruscan alphabet used only the Greek counterparts of the vowels "a," "e," "i" and "u." They dropped the "o" and did not use the consonants "d," "b" or "g." One confusing symbol, resembling a plus sign and once read as a "t," is now seen as a sign for a sibilant.

At first, would-be translators were baffled by the fact that Etruscan, like much early Greek, was virtually always written from right to left—the reverse of Latin and most modern languages in the West. In 600 B.C. the Greeks settled on a left-to-right script, and it was this system that Rome adopted. But the Etruscans never switched.

To confuse matters further, Etruscans on rare occasions wrote in a style called boustrophedon: "as the ox plows," going first right to left and then on the next line left to right. Also, they often wrote the beta (B), the sigma (S) and other letters backward.

Most of these peculiarities were recognized a century and a half ago, by which time scholars had managed to pick out about 50 Etruscan words and identify their meanings. Some were simple: letters that spelled out Aplu apparently referred to the Greek god Apollo; by the same logic, Hercle referred to the hero Herakles. But to translate some of the words, 19th Century linguists had to rely on what scholars call glosses, specific translations of Etruscan words written in Greek and Roman works. For example, the grammarian Hesychius of Alexandria, in the Fifth Century A.D., indicated that the Etruscan word *aisar*, found on many fragments, could be taken with some confidence to mean gods, and that *truna* meant power.

Such tiny clues help, but there simply are not enough of them. Nor is there sufficient variety in extant examples of Etruscan writing. More than 10,000 brief inscriptions have been found, but nearly all are funerary or dedicatory—written on tomb walls, sarcophagi, vases offered as gifts in temples and sanctuaries. They list names, titles, dates, gods and goddesses, and words for relationships. From them, scholars have managed to expand the known Etruscan vocabulary to about 200 basic words, plus a number of proper names.

The longest surviving text in Etruscan, found in the mid-1800s, was written on lengths of cloth wrapped around the mummified body of a woman. It contains some 1,300 words—many of them repetitions. The mummy it covered was bought in Egypt by a Croatian traveler who took it to his home in Vienna for inclusion in his private collection of antiquities. When the collector died, his purchase went to his native country—now Yugoslavia—and to the museum of Zagreb. There it was unwrapped, and to the astonishment of curators the long narrow strips of linen that had bound the body—bands four inches wide, some of them 10 feet long—turned out to be covered with Etruscan writing.

How a long Etruscan inscription came to be wrapped around an Egyptian mummy is one of the great riddles of scholarship, but its rather late date —around 100 B.C.—leads to the hypothesis that an Etruscan wanderer or soldier of fortune may have entered the service of one of the Ptolemaic rulers of Egypt after his native city had fallen to Rome. From the form and style of the writing, experts place the hypothetical Etruscan's home in north Etruria, perhaps in or near Clusium, the land of Lars Porsenna.

Perhaps the Etruscan took with him to Egypt both his wife and his most precious possession, one of the now-vanished, sacred Etruscan books. And when his wife died he yielded to local custom in the manner of wrapping her body—but substituted his own "holy book," cut into strips, in place of the conventional plain linen winding sheet.

The Linen Book is clearly a religious document. Most of it, written in red in a neat hand, is a repetitious list of gods and dates, and a calendar for the observance of sacred rites. There is also what seems to be an incantation. It begins: CEIA HIA-ETNAM CIZ VACL TRIN VALE. Attempts to understand the message have produced interpretations so wildly different that they would be funny—if the search for their meaning were not so serious. The opening phrase alone has been variously rendered—by zealous translators who were determined to confirm their theories —as "Shout energetically," "The fire has thrown out its gleams," "Call the shades of the fathers" and "Stride with frenzy."

The central reason why the Etruscan language still resists full comprehension after years of scholarly assault is that no extensive and sufficiently varied bilingual—that is, one passage rendered in two languages—has ever been found. An unknown language can be read with some assurance only if it can be compared with a like text in a readable language. The best-known example is the Rosetta stone, found in Egypt in 1799; it had three parallel inscriptions: in Greek, which was known, in Egyptian hieroglyphs and in a simplified Egyptian script called demotic. Thus it enabled the French philologist Jean-François Champollion to decipher the hieroglyphs.

Bronze mirrors engraved with pictures of Etruscan gods, and with names inscribed beside the figures (page 86), provide partial substitutes for a full bilingual. Since the gods portrayed can usually be correlated with Greek counterparts, it is reasonable to conclude, for instance, that Tinia is the same god as Zeus, only called by an Etruscan name. But the value of such comparisons is obviously limited—and the search for a full bilingual goes on.

In 1964 there was great excitement when the three folded gold sheets bearing Phoenician and Etruscan texts were discovered amid temple ruins in the ancient port of Pyrgi. But overly optimistic Etruscologists were disappointed. They hoped to match Etruscan phrases against Phoenician ones—which they had expected to read with ease—and thus determine what the Etruscan equivalents meant. However, the Phoenician version itself proved partially incomprehensible, so it could not serve as a good, straightforward guide to the Etruscan. Moreover, the two texts did not correspond word for word. And though the texts were quite lengthy, what scholars could translate consisted largely of a terse, unenlightening dedicatory formula. Finally, the supporting historical information required to analyze an unknown language was also missing. Thus the tablets could not provide the long-sought key.

The Pyrgi tablets did, however, make some contributions to knowledge of the language—and of Etruscan history. They confirmed that Uni and Astarte were the Etruscan and Phoenician names for the same goddess; also, scholars were able to isolate the verb "to give," and to establish the existence of a ruler named Thefarie Velianas and the length of time he ruled—three years.

An aerial photograph provides a spectacular perspective of
the Banditaccia necropolis, which was in use from 700 to 400
B.C. The largest of the 400 mound-covered tombs, at upper
right, is more than 100 feet in diameter. Opulent burial
chambers inside each grave were built of local sandstone.

Rectangular flat-topped tombs confront one another on a
well-ordered Banditaccia street. Unlike the tumulus tombs,
which sometimes housed the remains of generations, each
of these stone mausoleums held only one or two bodies.

A Well-planned City for the Dead

The passion of Etruscan aristocrats for an orderly and comfortable life after death prompted them to construct their burial sites with the same care given to building their cities. No Etruscan necropolis yet excavated is so impressive as the Banditaccia cemetery at Caere (opposite). It covers hundreds of acres, has streets and plazas, and a main road along which 2,500 or so years ago the rich were carried to their final resting place.

The tombs in which they were buried were furnished with a wealth of appurtenances that the dead souls might need. At first, the tombs were covered with mounds of earth called tumuli; some 200 years later, they were built like squat houses.

Calculations based on excavations of two sectors of the cemetery indicate the population of ancient Caere reached a prosperous peak of about 25,000 inhabitants during the Seventh and Sixth centuries B.C. The grandeur of the artifacts in the tombs, spanning Villanovan to Roman times, reinforces the possibility that Caere was the richest city in its world.

The so-called Tomb of the Shields and Chairs was robbed in ancient times and unscientifically explored by curious visitors in the 1800s. Both thieves and tourists took everything from the tomb that could be carried off—including objects that might have made it possible to identify the occupants. Only decorative stone shields and chairs, and the sarcophagi, remain.

Curiously, it was the word "three" that proved most interesting. Etruscan numbers—written out as words, not rendered as numerals—had long been a puzzle to scholars. Until the Pyrgi tablets were analyzed, only the Etruscan words for "one" and "two" were known; they read as *thu* and *zal*. From the tablets came the knowledge that "three" was *ci*. Small though this revelation may seem, it gave scholars the wherewithal to attack another mystery of long standing: how to understand a pair of dice that had turned up in a tomb at Tuscania in 1848.

Herodotus claimed that the Lydians, the Etruscans' putative forebears, had invented the game of dice—as well as knucklebones (a game like jacks) and certain ball sports. According to him, the Lydians played all day long every other day during the long period of famine that was ultimately to force them to emigrate. The purpose was to distract themselves from their empty stomachs; on the intervening days, they stopped such amusements and ate. But this account does not shed much light on how they played—or on how a throw of the dice was read.

Armed with their new knowledge of the word for "three," scholars applied it to their study of the Tuscania dice. Their six sides were incised not with dots or numerals, but with words. Etruscologists could read the words and knew the meaning of *thu, zal* and now *ci*. They surmised that the other three words —*huth, mach* and *sa*—meant four, five and six. But which was which?

One answer to the question—and a tentative one at that—rests on a mathematical guess that certain scholars have put forth. Their hunch, based on a notion that one of the words has a relative in Greek, is that Etruscan dice—like so many things Etruscan —are unusual. Most of the modern world's dice are made so that numbers on opposite sides add up to seven: one across from six, two across from five, three across from four. But the Etruscan system seems to have been different: their numbers apparently were paired to achieve a subtraction that always leaves three. By this arrangement, the four side would be opposite the one, the five opposite the two and the six opposite the three. From this logic, then, *huth* has been identified as four, *mach* as five and *sa*, six. So far that is everything known about Etruscan numbers—and even this has its doubters.

In the absence of a satisfactory key to Etruscan, scholars have decided to pick the linguistic lock like burglars—slowly, as silently as possible and in solitude. They concentrate less on trying to establish relationships with other languages and more on the evidence at hand—Etruscan inscriptions—whether limited bilinguals or writings on pictures and solid objects such as mirrors. This method has been yielding results that show promise of increasing the painfully small vocabulary of Etruscan words now known, but progress is slow.

Similarly, the search for geographical origins has shifted from seeking a foreign source to studying the historical development of Etruscans on the Italian peninsula. No matter what their origin, it was upon the soil of Italy that the Etruscans created their splendid civilization and achieved their historic position in the world. To spend too much time in the search for precise geographical origins and dates, says one Italian Etruscologist, is "like trying to establish the sex of angels. Let us be content with establishing the *existence* of angels."

Treasure Trove from a Rare Unplundered Tomb

Pottery figurines only four inches high stood guard over the dead in the great tomb; their arms are held in gestures of mourning.

Undiscovered by robbers over a period of some 2,600 years, the resting place of two Etruscan men and a woman of exalted station was opened for the first time in 1836. Named for its discoverers—a priest and a general—the Regolini-Galassi Tomb, near Caere, yielded an array of magnificent grave goods. Now displayed in the Vatican, the funerary finery has provided experts with much insight into the tastes and way of life of Seventh Century B.C. Etrurian aristocrats.

The source of their riches was the iron and copper ore that they traded briskly throughout the Mediterranean. They used their new affluence not only to delight the eyes of the living but to impress the gods and to furnish a luxurious afterlife.

Three distinct kinds of goods were found in the tomb. Some, such as the tiny votive figures above, were purely Etruscan in concept and execution. But the period, at the dawn of Etruria's rise, also saw an artistic explo-

sion that brought with it motifs from the Near East: sphinxes, lions and palmettes. Greek and western Asian artisans, drawn to Etruria's rich urban centers, spread these exotic themes over the Italic peninsula, and Etruscan patrons promptly took to them.

Imported works, brought by Phoenician and Greek traders, made up the third category. These pieces affirm that wealthy Etruscans drew on the entire Mediterranean world to enrich their own culture.

Showpieces of the Noble Estate

The surviving bronze trimmings of this full-sized chariot guided restorers in reconstructing its lost wooden parts. The vehicle, with 50-inch wheels, could carry two men. The shaft ends in a lion's head—a motif common in the Near East.

A fluted ceramic urn held the ashes of a man, the only cremated body in the Regolini-Galassi Tomb; the other two were laid out on biers. The funerary jar, made in the industrial city of Caere, had probably been commissioned by an ardent rider; an effigy of his horse —now headless—forms the lid's handle.

Set in the body of a four-wheeled hearse, a bed of bronze latticework on lotus-shaped legs carried the body of a warrior to his final rest. Probably during the funeral rites, the soldier's remains—still resting on the bed—were removed from the hearse. But the vehicle, decorated with Near Eastern designs, was entombed near him.

*Eight ceremonial shields of bronze like this one guarded the
dead warrior's soul in the grave. Though this shield
measures a yard across, it is so thin that now it must be held
together with a supportive backing of wire mesh.*

Household Effects for Eternity

A silver cup rimmed with a design of fish scales was found near a woman's remains. But the word Larthia scratched on the three-inch-high vessel may be her husband's name.

Probably an incense burner, this 40-inch wheeled bronze tray holds a bowl for charcoal. The work of an Etruscan smith, the piece is edged with lotus shapes inspired by Egyptian art.

Standing four feet high, a bronze cauldron atop a stand is incised with sphinxes now barely visible in the oxidized metal surface. Ferocious Greek griffins curve over the edge.

Phoenician traders brought this gilded
silver bowl from their colony on
Cyprus, probably as part payment for
unworked Etruscan metals. In the
center, two lions attack a bull. Circling
the scene, a man struggles with a
lion, and mounted and standing archers
twist to shower arrows on their prey.
On the outer band of the seven-inch-
wide basin, some soldiers carry spears
and shields; others drive chariots.
The designs are a blend, borrowed
from Egyptian and Syrian motifs.

Perhaps a holder for ivory or bronze
writing tools used to incise words on
wax tablets, this six-inch vase of
bucchero—a ware that was one
of Caere's chief products—is covered
with letters for students to copy.

Adornments for the Departed

A triad pattern of female deities is repeated several times on a four-inch-wide gold ornament—either an armlet or a massive earring—once worn by the woman in the tomb. The goddesses' fashions are a mix of styles: their coiffures are Egyptian, their flowing gowns are Greek-influenced.

The hollow rods and spheres of this three-strand golden necklace are covered with the geometric zigzags typical of Etruscan design. The necklace, which lacks two small pieces, draped 16 inches from its noble wearer's neck to fall to her waist.

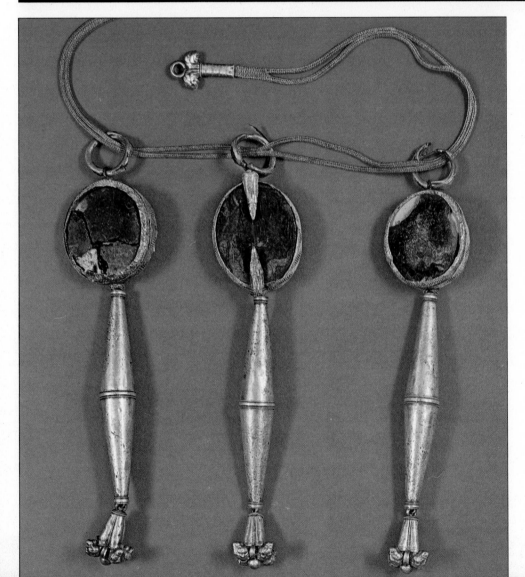

Like the ornament opposite, this breast pendant is heavy with granulation, a technique of affixing tiny gold beads to a gold background; Etruscan smiths excelled in the art. The inspiration for the female figures, who hold palm-leaf fans, came from Syria. The piece is about three inches wide at the top.

Amber from the Baltic Sea enriches nine-inch-long golden rods suspended from a mesh chain. Two lions' heads appear on the necklace's clasp, and on all three free-swinging tassels.

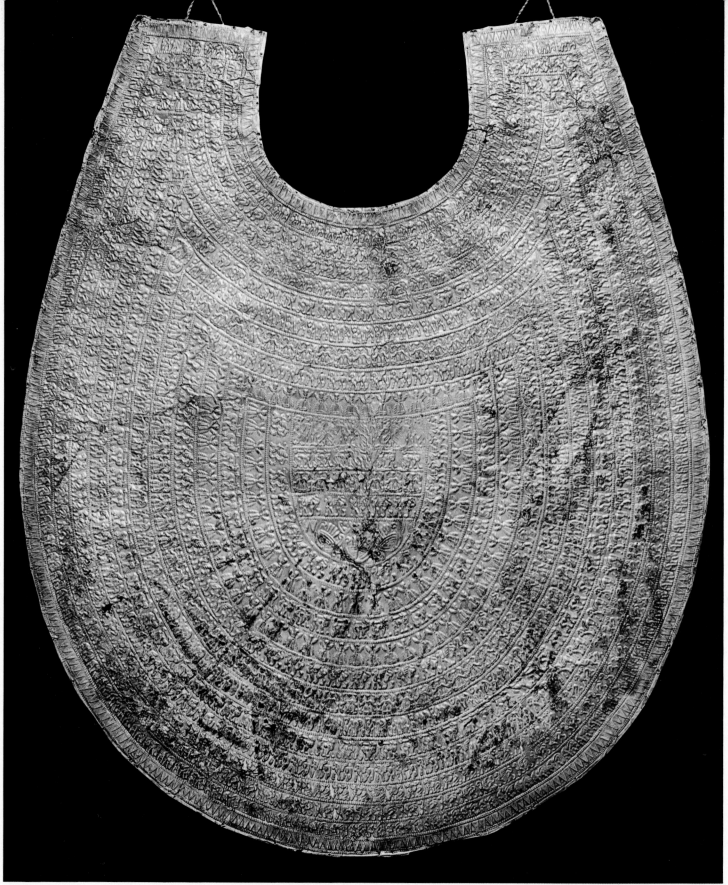

An overall pattern of many abstract designs, combined with those drawn from nature, covers this splendid 16-inch-high golden breastplate.

Pacing lions dominate a foot-high gold brooch. On the leaf-shaped lower pendant, lions in relief flank files of three-dimensional ducks.

For the aristocrats of Etruria, who left a record of their daily lives in the paintings and furnishings of their tombs, dusk was a combination of banquet time and show time. Toward sunset, on any given day toward the end of the Sixth Century B.C. in any Etruscan city, families and friends gathered in elegant houses to lie down for an evening of pleasure —dining on the choicest foods, drinking the finest wines, enjoying entertainment provided by gifted musicians and dancers who were retained as household servants. The nobles, men and women alike, counted on being treated to nothing but the best, because below them in society, masses of farmers, herders, vintners and craftsmen labored to make the lives of the privileged few supremely luxurious.

It is the close of a day and guests have arrived at the house of a highborn warrior. On the brightly painted walls of the dining chamber hang the host's bronze helmet and his breastplate, his iron-bladed swords, his shields and his javelins. On side tables stand several of his wife's most cherished possessions—handsome Greek ceramic vases decorated with mythological scenes in red against a black background. Candles in bronze candelabra light the room and the air is scented with burning incense. Since the evening is on the cool side, the room is warmed by charcoal fires smoldering in bronze braziers mounted on wheels—wares of the master metalsmiths of the city of Vulci.

Fashioned of terra cotta, a life-sized figure of an Etruscan noblewoman of the Second Century B.C. lounges on fringed cushions. Her luxuriant apparel and copious jewelry capture the Etruscans' passion for good living that shocked their austere Classical neighbors. With one hand she adjusts her veil; in the other—laden with rings—she holds a mirror.

The guests, in couples, recline side by side on cushioned banquet couches elevated above the floor on carved wooden feet. Servants dart about the chamber, rushing in and out from the kitchen. They carry great bronze platters heaped with fish and roasted pig, glossy black *bucchero* pottery bowls full of vegetables, gigantic cheeses and piles of fruit. Some of the servants bring wine goblets and carafes, painted in the Greek style, filled with water to dilute the Etruscan wine, which is heavy and sweet. Food and drink are placed on low double-tiered tables alongside the reclining diners, who reach with long, graceful fingers to select choice morsels. Soon pet dogs and household geese are battling for scraps that have fallen to the floor, and the dogs snarl at each other over mouthfuls of meat rejected by the pampered diners as too tough to chew. Wine goblets are raised in frequent toasts; sometimes, before touching the cups to their lips, the diners brush from the rims a bee drawn by the wine's sweetness.

The women are languorous, light-skinned, heavy-lidded. They wear eye make-up, their lips are rouged and their hair is drawn back and piled high in the Etruscan style—an upswept bun that several of the women have covered with a shawl of patterned woolen fabric. They are decked in gold earrings, bracelets and necklaces. Their colorful linen tunics, worn low on their shoulders so as to leave their long necks bare, are belted and fall in graceful folds to the ankles.

The reclining men do not appear to be much taller than the women—and indeed their average height is only about five feet, four inches. The younger men are clean-shaven and wear their dark, curly hair cropped short—another fashion recently adopted from the Greeks. One of the older men, however, still wears the traditional Etruscan beard and long hair of generations past.

A few of the men wear cloaks—the Greeks and Romans called them *tebennae*—draped over one shoulder. The garment is a semicircular piece of woolen fabric woven of strong colors. Some designs are solid tones bordered with a contrasting hue; others incorporate figured patterns. But in the warmth of the braziers, most of the men have slipped their *tebennae* off their shoulders and wear them tucked loosely around their midriffs; they are bare to the waist. (In years to come the Romans will adopt the *tebenna* and transform it into the toga, worn to designate Roman citizenship.)

On low foot benches beside the couches some of the diners have placed their shoes, of which they are inordinately proud. Nobody else in the world of the Sixth Century B.C. has more elegant footwear. Made of fine black or red leather, they curl to a point at the toes; some fit high up the back of the calf and lace across the front of the ankle.

Around and behind and between the dining couches move musicians and dancers—slaves in the household of the host. Virile young men wearing woven wreaths of flowers on their heads play on the long double pipe that is the Etruscans' favorite instrument (page 77). Others strum the lyre. The musicians are scantily clad, wearing only brightly colored, scarflike garments draped from shoulder to knee. Dancers of both sexes prance in patterned duets, their arms raised high and fingers extended outward and upward in accent to the music; some of the women click castanets.

Gaming boards resembling those for chess or backgammon are brought out between courses, and ivory dice rattle. Plates clatter. There is loud talk and laughter. The musicians tootle and strum. Servants quarrel in the courtyard. The dogs bark and the geese hiss. It is very noisy when wealthy Etrurians entertain at dinner, but always merry.

The wall paintings in Etruscan tombs show many such convivial dinners of 2,500 years ago in elaborate detail (pages 78-79). Corroborating this pictorial evidence, several Classical authors recorded the lavish scale of Etruscan dining. The Greek philosopher and traveler Posidonius, writing in the Second Century B.C., observed that the Etruscans had tables "sumptuously laid with everything that can contribute to delicate living; they have couch coverings embroidered with flowers and are served from quantities of silver dishes; and they have at their beck and call a considerable number of slaves."

Other writers spoke of the Etruscans' love of music, which accompanied nearly every activity from private festivities to funerals and religious rituals. This passion astounded their contemporaries. According to some accounts, the Etruscans fought their battles, beat their slaves, even kneaded their bread to the rhythm of music (a fresco in a tomb near Orvieto shows a piper tootling away while a baker mixes a batch of dough).

Did the Etruscans sing to their music? Apparently not. The historian Livy, writing about Etruscan soothsayers and entertainers who were invited to Rome around 365 B.C. to appease the gods and drive away a plague, reported that "players from Etruria, dancing to the sound of the pipe, executed in the Tuscan manner certain movements that were not without grace, but they did not accompany them with either songs or actions."

Larger than life, terra-cotta effigies of a young patrician couple recline on the lid of their joint sarcophagus, made around 500 B.C. Stretched on a banquet couch, his arm tenderly encircling her shoulder, they seem engaged in animated conversation. The lady has adopted a Grecian gown and cap, but the custom of men and women consorting publicly in easy familiarity is wholly Etruscan; Greek women were kept very much in the background.

If the Etruscans did not sing, they certainly danced (pages 80-81). They dance all over the walls of tombs, on vases, on bas-reliefs, on mirrors. They danced as entertainers at banquets, as soldiers in rituals to invoke the favor of the gods of war, as participants in rites on nonmartial occasions. They danced in a simple effusion of high spirits and good health, and of the joy of living in the bright Etruscan sun.

The houses in which much of this activity took place can be reconstructed partly from the remains of dwellings excavated by archeologists; but again, the primary source of information is the Etruscan tombs, whose designs generally were faithful copies of the form and detail of their owners' actual homes. The main difference is that the resting places of the dead were wholly or partially carved into rock, while those of the living were made of sun-dried mud brick on a frame of heavy timbers—of oak, for instance, or beech—cut from the forests that were abundant in the Italy of Etruscan days.

Recent Swedish excavations of an Etruscan city at Acquarossa, near Viterbo, have confirmed the similarities between the Etruscans' homes and their tombs. At Acquarossa a fairly standard house of an Etruscan aristocrat of around 550 B.C. seems to have been a rectangular, single-story structure that might measure 30 by 40 feet, set upon a foundation of tufa blocks. The pitched roof was covered with terracotta tiles, some as large as three feet long and 18 inches wide. The roof extended well beyond the house walls in order to protect the bricks and timbers from rain. The gables and eaves were sometimes as elaborately ornamented as those of the temples (pages 102-107), with brightly painted terra-cotta reliefs of animals and monsters as well as purely decorative, abstract designs. All the doors and windows were framed by sturdy timber posts and lintels.

The ground plan of a typical Acquarossa house, like close counterparts at other Etruscan sites, was quite simple. One approached through a broad walled courtyard that was open to the sky. Across the court, the visitor arrived at the entrance to the house's vestibule—a roofed room measuring only a few feet from front to back but as wide as the house itself. This hall may have been where merchants delivered provisions, a passageway for servants going about their business and even a place where people —again, probably servants—slept. In Roman architecture this room may have evolved into the atrium, which was a reception area for merchants, business associates and guests. According to the Roman his-

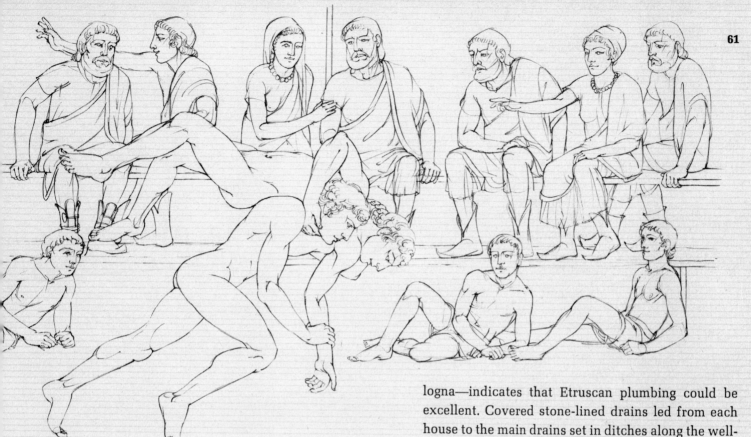

torian Varro, the Romans inherited the idea of the atrium—and its name—from the Etruscans.

On the far side of the vestibule were doors that gave access to three rooms, lined up side by side across the width of the house. The center room —probably not much more than 15 feet wide—did multiple service. By day the master of the house probably transacted business here. But at night it turned into a dining and entertainment hall; at the close of evening, when the parties were over, the room's banquet couches served as beds for the hosts and any guests too tipsy to wend their way home.

One of the side rooms was a general workplace and kitchen, with a combination oven and open hearth; the other served either as a second bedroom or for storage. Where the various members of the family slept is uncertain; there is no evidence that they were segregated by generation, but parents most likely reserved the privacy of the center room for themselves.

Evidence from another site—Marzabotto, near Bo-

logna—indicates that Etruscan plumbing could be excellent. Covered stone-lined drains led from each house to the main drains set in ditches along the well-tamped, pebble-paved streets. Other conduits, made of cylindrical terra-cotta pipes and molded to fit into each other as efficiently as modern pipe sections, brought in clean water by gravity from nearby elevated cisterns. Many houses also had their own stone-lined wells within their courtyards.

Of the interior fittings and the utensils of an Etruscan home virtually nothing has been found aboveground except bits and pieces of household crockery. But the tombs, as always, tell much. Some have yielded actual objects placed in the burial chambers as gifts to the dead and as the furnishings for feasts in the afterlife: bronze candelabra, dishes, trays, wine vessels, strainers, cups, tables, chairs. Other tombs reveal a full array of household equipment in wall paintings or terra-cotta bas-reliefs.

For many Classical observers, the Etruscan style of life was far too lavish—and too hedonistic—to suit their more reserved tastes. One aspect that came under frequent attack was the Etruscans' alleged easy way in sexual matters. They went about much of their daily—as well as nocturnal—business in mixed pairs;

"Skilled and Loving Craftsmen"

The talent and sophistication of Etruscan artisans, who were much valued by their own countrymen, eventually impressed even the usually disdainful Greeks. Possibly the respect developed because the Etruscans adapted Greek mythological themes to their ornamental motifs. In any case, the Fifth Century B.C. Greek poet Pherecrates warmly referred to Etruria's "skilled and loving craftsmen."

These esteemed artisans used a variety of metal and clay materials. Etruria's wealth of both tin and copper—the main components of bronze—made that alloy widely available for weapons, for furnishings and for decorative uses; Etruscan ladies kept their make-up, hairpins and combs in bronze boxes called *cistae (right)*.

The Etruscans also specialized in *bucchero pottery (far right)*, whose characteristic black color was obtained by firing the indigenous clay, which contained in it some iron, in a unique process that served to combine oxygen with the iron to form a black ferrous oxide.

The cista at right, a vanity case more than two feet high and 13 inches in diameter, was made in Praeneste, near Rome, in 350 B.C. The engravings on it illustrate a Greek legend in which a hero named Polydeuces binds the pugnacious King Amycus to a tree as punishment for forcing strangers to box with him. An approving witness is the goddess Athena (center) dressed in high Etruscan style. On the lid stand the wine god Dionysus and two satyrs.

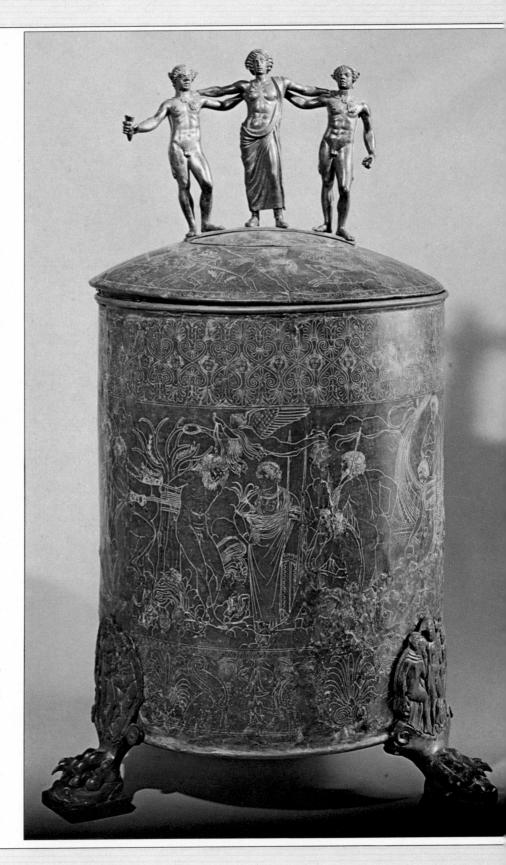

An exquisite Seventh Century B.C. gold
wine cup, less than four inches high,
was taken from the Bernardini Tomb in
Praeneste. Stylized sphinxes from
Greek mythology—monstrous figures
with lions' bodies and human heads
—adorn the wine cup's handles.

This 18-inch bucchero vase from
Orvieto is 2,600 years old. Both Greek
and Etruscan artisans often based their
designs on Eastern motifs; for this
work, the horse surmounting the vase
and the band of repeated dogs were
drawn from that foreign influence.

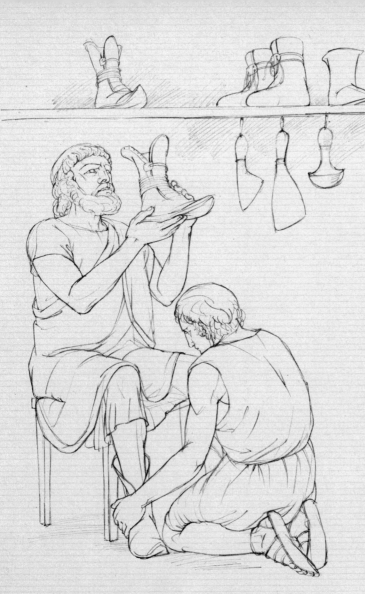

and while, in a world of couples, some coupling can be expected, to Greek and Roman eyes the Etruscans carried the habit beyond the limits of decency.

For example, the gossipy Greek historian Theopompus, writing in the Fourth Century B.C., reported of the Etruscans that: "There is no shame for them to be seen committing a sexual act in public. And so removed are they from regarding the act as shameful that when the master of the house is engaged in making love and he is called for, they"—presumably his servants—"say: 'He is doing so-and-so,' referring to the act quite impudently by its name. When there are gatherings of family or friends, this is how they do: first of all, when they have finished drinking and are ready for bed and while the torches are still lighted, the servants bring in sometimes courtesans, some-

times handsome boys, sometimes their own wives."

Warming to his subject, Theopompus went on to say that Etruscan women were accustomed to exercise naked, to wax their bodies to remove hair (a practice he considered disgusting), to make love with anyone who asked and to "bring up together all those children that are born to them, heedless of who their fathers may be."

But Theopompus must be taken with a grain of salt. Even in his own time he was regarded as a writer with a poisoned pen, and beyond that general failing he was, in this instance, writing within the framework of a long-standing Greek dislike for his subjects as a people. It was the Etruscans, after all, who had made common cause with Carthage to block Greece at sea; it was the Etruscans who had halted the Greek advance up the Italian peninsula beyond Cumae.

Whether or not Theopompus was accurate with the facts, his bias often led him to ignore obvious implications. For example, it is hard to believe that married Etruscan women brought up numbers of children born to them by various sires without the concurrence of their husbands.

The essential point behind Theopompus' observation—the thing that really bothered him—was less the alleged licentiousness of Etruria's women, or their disregard for what other cultures measured as propriety, than their near-equality with men. The freedom they enjoyed shocked Greek and Roman writers. Scandalized, they reported that these females were not restricted to quiet chambers like the Greek women's quarters, nor were they expected to pass all their time instructing children and weaving cloth as did virtuous Roman matrons. Instead they appeared in plain view, openly eating and drinking with their husbands, extending their wine goblets to waiting servants for refilling whenever they wished and even proposing toasts to guests. Quite a difference from the role imposed on Roman wives, who not only were forbidden to drink wine in the first place but who were—at least at one time—required to kiss their husbands' male relatives chastely upon the cheek each day to prove their breath was uncontaminated by alcohol.

There seems no doubt that Etruscan women did indeed enjoy many of the privileges Theopompus and his colleagues complained about. There is evidence, for example, that they freely attended public spectacles, including sporting events; paintings in tombs at Orvieto and Tarquinii show them eagerly watching boxers, acrobats and racing charioteers.

Theopompus simply didn't understand that it was possible for women to be treated as equal to men without being promiscuous. In contradiction to his portrait of a loose-living, careless people is the image of Etruscan couples that emerges from funerary inscriptions on sarcophagi. It is a picture of evenly matched partners at the head of affectionate father-mother-children family units.

Of course, all was not sweetness and light in every Etruscan household. A tale that comes down from Rome during the First Century A.D. relates how one Plautius Silvanus, a prominent young Etruscan living in Rome, threw his wife out the window one night in the course of a family argument. But such a breach of domestic harmony left a stain on the family name that was intolerable to Plautius' grandmother, a harridan named Urgulania. Urgulania tried to right the wrong by presenting a dagger to Plautius with which

he was supposed to take his own life. But he did not.

As a last resort, Urgulania—by chance, a close friend of Livia, wife of the Roman Emperor Augustus—connived to get Plautius out of the house by an alternate arrangement. She managed to have her grandson the wife-thrower appointed companion to Livia's grandson—a young man the imperial family considered to be a near-idiot. Perhaps at the time, Urgulania and Livia thought their problem grandsons deserved each other. But the wife-thrower proved to be a good tutor and the near-idiot a good scholar. The latter became steeped in knowledge of Etruscan ways and lore, and grew up to become the intellectual Emperor Claudius, author of the 20 now-lost volumes devoted to the history of the Etruscans.

While not all Etruscan women were as influential as Urgulania, they were certainly all persons in their own right with names—and minds—of their own. Even the most prominent of Roman women was known only by the feminine form of her father's family name—Claudia for Claudius, Tullia for Tullius, Cornelia for Cornelius. But Etruscan women had first names of their own as well as family names.

A number of these given names have survived on objects found in tombs, confirming that Etruscan matrons had property rights as well. For example, in one tomb noted for its rich yield of Greek ware, archeologists found the vases signed not only by the potter who made them but also inscribed with the names of their Etruscan owners. "I belong to Culni," says one. Another reports "I am the property of Ati." Various family funerary inscriptions refer to Veilia, to Anneia, to Coesidia, to Ramtha, to Tanaquil.

It was a Tanaquil who became the best-known and most clearly identified Etruscan woman to emerge as

A Guide to the Tomb of the Reliefs

Because Etruscans believed that the dead had the same wants as the living, they equipped graves with all the needs and comforts of earthly existence. For this reason their excavated tombs often provide accurate reflections of how Etruscan households looked. The Tomb of the Reliefs at Cerveteri is probably the best example of a burial place that fully evokes the atmosphere of a dwelling.

The worldly goods in this rock-hewn chamber are provided in symbolic form as bas-reliefs of stucco that once were brightly painted. Cooking utensils, tools and crockery —all the standard equipment of a prosperous Third Century B.C. home—are neatly disposed over the tomb's great, square supporting columns. The weaponry that would be hanging in a highborn warrior's house is displayed on the walls. Two beds with plump pillows seem ready for sleepers. By one couch—decorated with a relief of Charun, the ferryman of myth, and his dog Cerberus —a pair of lady's slippers rests on a low bench. The tomb's only extraneous object is an external grave marker *(center, foreground)*, which archeologists brought in.

Plaster images of articles used in the daily life of a rich Etruscan family cover the surfaces in the Tomb of the Reliefs. The items—as well as two household pets—are identified below.

1. Shepherd's crook	12. Folded linen
2. Wine jug	13. Linen chest
3. Drinking bowl	14. Decorated bed
4. Cutlass	15. Helmet and shields
5. Pickax	16. Sandals on foot bench
6. Coil of rope	17. Pestle
7. Wheeled table	18. Basin on tripod
8. Knapsack	19. Ladle
9. Goose	20. Knife rack
10. Marten	21. Roasting spits
11. Pillows	22. Wheel of cheese

a historical figure. The wife of the man who, under the Latinized name of Lucius Tarquinius, became the first Etruscan ruler of Rome, she seems to have been a formidable lady indeed. If the saga of Tanaquil and her husband, as told by Livy, is even in small part correct, she played a major role in Tarquinius' rise to kingship and the establishment of Etruscans on the Roman throne.

According to Livy, Tanaquil was a member of the aristocracy in Tarquinii and resented the way her fellow citizens looked down on her husband, whose mother had been Etruscan but whose father was an immigrant Greek. She was, as Livy told it, "not of a sort to put up with humbler circumstances in her married life than those she had previously been accustomed to. Wholly bent upon seeing her husband enjoy the respect he deserved, she smothered all feeling of natural affection for her native town and determined to abandon it forever. For the purpose she had in mind she decided that the most suitable place was Rome. Rome was a young and rising community; there would be opportunities for a courageous man in a place where all advancement came swiftly."

Thus, says Livy, at Tanaquil's urging the two went off to Rome by carriage, probably about 625 B.C. (Some modern scholars think her husband may well have been riding not in a carriage but in the lead of a freelancing, freebooting army.) They arrived at the summit of the Janiculum Hill, which commands a splendid view of the Tiber River as well as the low, flat area that became the site of the Forum, and of the modest heights the world calls the Seven Hills. On top of the Janiculum, Tanaquil and her spouse paused—probably gaping, as have many of the millions who have followed them to this highest point in Rome. Suddenly an eagle swooped to the head of Tanaquil's husband, snatched off his cap, flew off with it, then circled and replaced it.

"Tanaquil, like most Etruscans, was well skilled in celestial prodigies," wrote Livy, "and joyfully accepted the omen. Flinging her arms round her husband's neck, she told him that no fortune was too high to hope for. 'Only consider,' she cried, 'from what quarter of the sky the eagle came! Did it not declare its message by coming to your *head*—the highest part of you? Did it not take the crown, as it were, from a human head, only to restore it, by heaven's approval, where it belongs?' "

Livy goes on to tell how Tarquinius—helped by Tanaquil's ambition and omen reading, plus his own enthusiasm and canvassing for votes—was elected to the Roman throne in 616 B.C. After seeing her husband made king, Tanaquil proceeded to find and elevate his successor, a young Etruscan whose Romanized name was Servius Tullius *(pages 27-29)*, and to manage his career.

Livy again: "The little boy was lying asleep, when his head burst into flames. The noise and excitement caused by such an extraordinary event came to the ears of the king and queen, and brought them hurrying to the spot. A servant ran for water and was about to throw it on the flames, when the queen stopped him, declaring that the child must on no account be disturbed. Tanaquil took her husband aside and said, 'He will one day prove a light in our darkness, a prop to our house in the day of its affliction.' "

In time she married the boy to her daughter. Then, when assassins murdered Tarquinius, she made sure that Servius Tullius succeeded him. Though her husband was dead, Tanaquil went to a window of the pal-

The garden of an Etruscan home is the setting for this Fourth Century B.C. game, probably an early form of backgammon, played with dice on a board called a tabula lusoria. Instead of spots, each die face bore written numbers; apparently when values of paired opposite faces were subtracted, the result was always three: six minus three, five minus two, four minus one, etc. The woman wears a mantle over her tunic, or chiton, and highly ornamented gold earrings. The man is dressed in a tebenna, or short rounded cloak, and leather sandals.

ace and assured the alarmed populace that the king had only been incapacitated by a blow on the head. Everything would be all right, she said, but until the king was fully recovered, Servius Tullius as his deputy would sit on the throne. It was done—and by the time the Roman public learned that the king had actually died, Servius Tullius was in full possession of the monarchy.

But Etruscan fate—left in the hands of women—took a tragic turn. The strong-willed Tanaquil, said Livy, was succeeded by another determined lady: Servius Tullius' daughter Tullia, who, along with her gentler-tempered sister, had been married off to sons of Tanaquil and Tarquinius. But if Tanaquil had anything to do with arranging the marriages, in this instance her usual keen judgment deserted her. The couples could not have been more poorly matched. One son and one sister were meek, their mates tough and ambitious. The willful Tullia got the wrong husband—the meek one—and she coveted her sister's more aggressive spouse. So she connived to have both her sister and her own husband murdered; she married the dead sister's husband, and then helped to plot the killing of her father, the king. The assassination accomplished, she ordered her carriage driven over his bloody body and saw her new husband Lucius Tarquinius Superbus crowned king; he was the man whose arrogance led in 509 B.C. to his overthrow as the last of Rome's Tarquin rulers.

If Livy's account is to be accepted, Tullia had served her Etruscan countrymen badly; her recklessness ultimately cost them the Roman throne. Rome itself could not have produced a better *saboteuse*.

Despite the ruthless politicking of Tanaquil and Tullia, most Etruscan women were intensely femi-

Trinkets Wrought in Gold

As might be expected of a rich people in love with display, the Etruscan upper classes adorned themselves lavishly with jewels, particularly ornaments of gold. The metal was fashioned into wreaths, pendants, bracelets, breastplates and large clasps or fibulae.

The Etruscans imported gold ore from Africa and Asia, then turned it over to local metalsmiths. However, some craftsmen may have immigrated from the East, bringing with them the Near Eastern styles characteristic of much Etruscan finery. Highly skilled, these smiths became masters of the technique of granulation, by which tiny gold particles are soldered onto a background to create sparkling auras of reflected light. It was this technique that allowed Etruscan jewelers to fashion such intricate finished works as the pendant at right and the clasp on the opposite page.

A gold pendant less than two inches high represents the head of the horned river god Achelous; it was crafted in 500 B.C. Tiny gold spheres make up the hair and beard framing the face.

Wrought in the Third Century B.C., this nine-inch wreath of fragile gold oak leaves comes from Vulci. It was probably worn as a tiara.

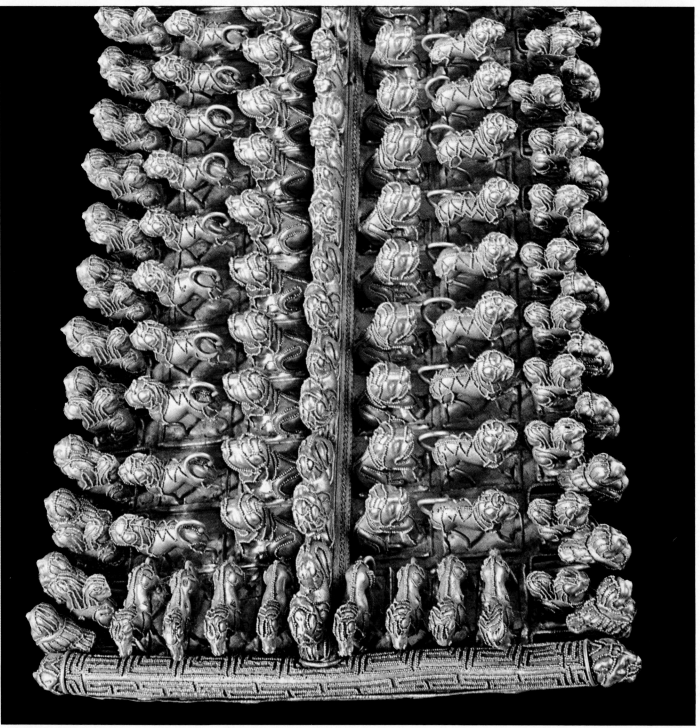

In a display of virtuosity, the Seventh Century B.C. artisan
who made this clasp, probably for a wide belt, covered a
five-by-seven-inch plaque with scores of creatures, including
lions and sirens. He embellished their details with gold
granules and used the same technique on the tubular frame.

nine. They delighted in personal adornments. Their fineries, including gold jewelry of exquisite workmanship, turn up in family tombs alongside the prized possessions of their husbands. In life, these priceless fripperies were kept in coffers of wood or bronze, which served as combination jewel cases and toilette kits that held materials for applying lipstick and eye shadow. The effect these women must have created, when their make-up was on and their jewels in place, must have been dazzling. And it was not lost on the ladies themselves, to judge from the enormous number of handsome polished bronze hand mirrors buried with them.

Beyond demonstrating a love of self-adornment and of their own visages, these Etruscan mirrors provide a subtle index of the ladies' level of sophistication. Many are engraved with mythological figures and bear inscriptions that identify the characters or even describe the scene *(pages 86 and 94)*. It would have been pointless, of course, to put an inscription on a mirror if its owner could neither read nor appreciate its references.

Did the Etruscan women wear their finest possessions about the house, or did they reserve them for high religious or family occasions? The guess is that they dressed up routinely, because clothes and jewels have always been designed as much to satisfy personal vanity as to demonstrate status and power.

Some observers were so awe-struck by the overdressing, overeating, overspending of the Etruscan rich that they failed to notice—or at least to report—other fascinating details. Posidonius, for one, went on at great length about the table settings and other lavish accouterments of Etruscan diners, but said almost nothing about what the banqueters ate. Nor did

he shed much light on the "great crowds of servants" who provided and served the delicacies on which the wealthy dined so lavishly.

Little is known about the hardworking souls in Etruria who produced food, or the thousands who sailed the ships, fought the battles, mined the ore and performed all the daily tasks that created and sustained the wealth of the cities. By and large, the masses of people who made up Etruria's labor force remain faceless and nameless.

Clearly a vast social gap existed between the ruling class and the masses who supported it. This was true of many societies contemporary with Etruria, but there is some indication that Etruscan servants and slaves were treated well. Posidonius did report, with a tinge of disapproval, that they "dress themselves in clothes more magnificent than befits their station of servitude, and the domestic staff have all kinds of private dwellings."

Though there was no middle class in modern terms, there was a special stratum called the *etera*—the equivalent of the Roman *clientes:* persons who stood somewhere between the ranks of lords and slaves, and who performed ordinary tasks or special services for their patrons. In return for total loyalty and assistance, the *etera* were given protection—and sometimes the right to be buried in the family tombs of the men they served.

Livy presented a vignette that casts some sidelong light on the role of the *etera.* The story involved the brave Roman soldier Gaius Mucius, who attempted to assassinate Lars Porsenna, the Etruscan king of Clusium, when that ruler laid siege to Rome in 509 B.C. According to Livy, Gaius Mucius managed to

A fluted bronze saucer, probably used to burn oil or resin for lighting on festive occasions, perches atop an arabesque sprouting from a girl's head. She dances on a pedestal supported by three legs, each decorated with a monster's head and a leonine paw. The lamp, less than 15 inches tall, was made in the Third Century B.C.

penetrate the Etruscan camp where "he took his stand in the crowd close to the raised platform where the king was sitting. By the side of the king sat his secretary, very busy; he was dressed much like his master, and, as most of the men addressed themselves to him, Mucius could not be sure which was the secretary and which the king."

In the end Mucius took a chance—and stabbed the wrong man: the secretary. But the interesting part of the tale to the historians is that a Roman could not distinguish, from dress or manner, between an Etruscan king and his Etruscan secretary.

Among the jobs members of the *etera* could perform was the management of farms owned by nobles. In the capacity of tenant farmer they could keep for their own needs some of the products of their labors. As a result, some of the *etera* in time grew wealthy enough to buy a shield and a sword, and go off to fight Etruria's battles as the equivalent of the Greek hoplite, the self-armed citizen-infantryman of the Greek city-states.

While the farmers of Etruria are only shadowy figures, there is considerable information about what they raised, chiefly for the benefit of their masters.

Raising pigs appears to have been among their specialties. Polybius, a Third Century B.C. Greek historian, told how swineherds near the Tyrrhenian seacoast walked huge numbers of the animals up and down the beaches. The Etruscans walked *ahead* of their pigs, like parade marshals, instead of driving them from behind. Every now and then the farmer would blow a blast on a trumpet—a sound the pigs had learned to recognize and follow.

The Etruscans' way with music seems to have had its influence on wild, as well as on domesticated, an-

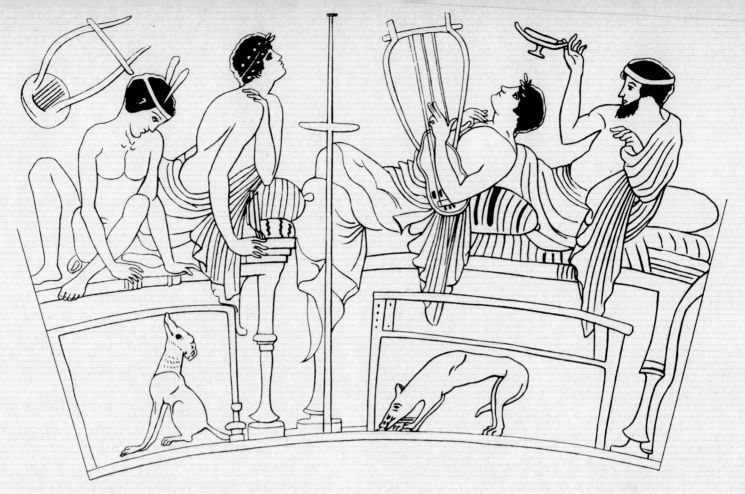

imals. In a curious passage from his *History of the Animals,* written in the Third Century A.D., the Roman author Aelian revived a story of how Etruscans used music in the hunt:

"It is said that in Etruria, where wild pigs and stags are caught with nets and dogs in the usual manner, success is greater when music is used as an aid. Nets are stretched out and all kinds of traps set in position. Along comes an experienced piper. He plays the sweetest tunes the double pipe can produce. In the silent solitude, his airs float up into all the retreats and breeding grounds of the game. At first the animals are terrified. But later they are irresistibly overcome by the enjoyment of the music. Enraptured, they are gradually attracted by the powerful music and they draw near, bewitched by the sounds, until they fall, overpowered, into the snares."

In addition to their great herds of pigs, Etruscan farmers also had domesticated cattle, goats, sheep, ducks, geese and chickens. The cattle were sometimes used for food—at least by the farmers' over-

lords—as well as for pulling plows and wagons.

From the milk of the farmers' ewes the Etruscans made cheeses, including a delicious variety that is still produced—thank the gods—in Tuscany, where it is called Pecorino. In the northern Etruscan town of Luni, tradition says, such cheeses were made in enormous wheels that could weigh as much as a thousand pounds each.

Etruria was rich in cereal grains, including barley, millet and several varieties of wheat. Many ancient writers referred to Etruscan orchards, but they did not explain precisely what kind of fruit was grown. Tomb paintings, however, show apples, blackberries and pomegranates—although their representation may have been borrowed from Greek art and so does not necessarily prove that the fruits were actually grown in Etruria. It is also possible that the pomegranates were purely symbolic; they were a widespread fertility symbol in ancient Greece and much of Italy. Similarly, funerary art includes vegetables —particularly artichokes, which are native to Italy

Etruscan banqueters were particularly fond of a target-hitting game called kottabos. The object was to upset a small disk balanced atop a pole (center), thus producing a satisfying "ping" as it struck the bronze basin beneath. Wine was the usual missile, either spat forcefully, as one tipsy reveler (second from left) is about to do in this drawing from a vase painting, or hurled—with a practiced flip of the wrist—from a cup hooked on the thumb (figure at far right). The man at the far left gazing at a dog may be out of range, but the bemused lute player is a potential target in the cross fire.

and still rank among the important Italian crops.

But the grape—as fruit and for wine making—was certainly raised in Etruria. Etruscan wines became known as far away as Greece and Spain.

Surprisingly, for a region whose hills today are feathery with the skittering, twittering gray-green leaves of olive groves, the cultivated olive seems to have been unknown in Etruria. Etruscans imported olive oil from Greece; fragments of the vases in which it was shipped lie scattered over many Etruscan sites.

Although many of the products raised in Etruscan fields and orchards cannot be identified, the implements used by Etruscan farmers can be. Some of the actual tools, mostly of iron, have been found; others are known from counterparts in bronze that served as votive offerings, and from representations in tombs. These implements differ hardly at all from many still to be seen in some remote areas of rural Italy. Among them are hoes, spades, sickles, pruning hooks, picks, shovels, assorted knives and several kinds of wood and metal plows—crude ones that the farmer had to drag across a field to make a furrow, and more sophisticated ones that could be drawn by a yoked ox or by a team. Though all these are elementary tools, they seem to have been sufficient to help Etruscan farmers extract remarkable wealth from their soil.

Further, and fascinating, light on Etruscan farm life comes from the Etruscan agronomist Saserna who, toward the close of the Second Century B.C., produced a written volume on farming methods. Along with most Etruscan literature, his original work has vanished, but parts of it survive in references by Varro, Pliny and other Roman authors.

Among other things, Saserna described an insec-

ticide, one of his own invention and guaranteed to give satisfactory results. "Take a root of serpentaria [an aromatic vine]," he advised, "and let it soak in water, then pour the water over the place you wish to disinfect; no bug will come near it." And if perchance the bugs deserted the fields for a less hostile environment in the farmer's house, Saserna had a remedy for that too. The farmer should "mix ox's gall with vinegar, and rub the bed with this."

Saserna also offered some helpful hints that must have been of great interest to a farmer's wife, especially if she was troubled with unwanted hair. A yellow tree frog boiled in water, he claimed, made an excellent depilatory. After boiling had reduced the frog to less than half its size, rubbing the afflicted part of the body with it would leave the skin clear and smooth. This odd-sounding balm may have been one of the beauty treatments used by the elegant ladies of Etruria's cities.

For a people who left no writings of their own to describe their lavish way of life, a surprising amount is known about the character and behavior of the Etruscan ruling class. But exactly what these luxury-loving aristocrats looked like is another question. In some cases tomb paintings show the women with light skin and blonde hair; the disproportionate number of blondes suggests that many lightened their hair with bleach. The men usually have dark hair and reddish sun-bronzed skin. Frescoes from the Sixth to the First Century B.C. show noses ranging from prominently aquiline to small and pert; some of the figures have the Classical straight nose with no indentation above the bridge.

There is no way of knowing, however, just how accurate such depictions may be. Artistic conventions certainly determined to some extent how Etruscan painters portrayed their subjects—and the period of the late Sixth and early Fifth centuries B.C. was a time when the art style of the Greeks in Asia Minor, the Ionians, was adopted both in Athens and in Etruria. The people in Etruscan tombs then were painted in accordance with that Ionian style: with curving mouths, almond-shaped eyes, long-fingered, supple hands and long slender feet—the better, perhaps, to show off the shoes of which they were so proud. Furthermore, the portraiture probably was idealized, as well as influenced by the fashion of the period. Still, Etruscan painters loved to capture realistic details and local color, so many of these lively men and women may have been portrayed very much as they actually looked in life.

Early sarcophagus lids, upon which sculptors created portraits of the dead, repeat details of the tomb paintings—the same slanting, wide-set eyes, the same long-fingered hands. Later on they demonstrate a greater dedication to realism: the bodies range from lithe to paunchy, and the features from fine and aristocratic to furrowed and coarse.

Modern scientists—armed with these pictorial and sculptural records, with Etruscan skeletons and with information from epitaphs about age at time of death —have struggled mightily to reconstruct the physical traits of the Etruscan people. But all this assiduous study has yielded few conclusions other than the fact that there was wide variety. For example, an attempt to establish a possible Eastern origin of the Etruscan people by comparing their skulls with those of the dominant long-headed type found in Near Eastern graves yielded only confusion. Of 44 Etruscan skulls taken from seven different sites, 34 turned out to be a near-equal mixture of long-headed and medium-headed types, and 10 were short-headed. (Other bone studies have provided less equivocal information of another kind: evidence that Etruscan dentists had acquired sophisticated skills. Some skulls from Tarquinii and other sites had teeth crowned and bridged with light, tight gold fittings. In a few cases the bridgework held human or animal teeth in substitution for ones that had been lost.)

French Etruscologist Jacques Heurgon, recapitulating all the evidence—scientific, artistic and literary —in the search for an Etruscan type, concluded that Etruscans looked like "Tuscan peasants, condottieri, Roman priests and emperors, young Bonapartes; and, on an urn from Volterra which shows us two happy sixty-year-olds, we might be looking at Ovid's Philemon and Baucis."

The Etruscans were, in sum, as varied a mixture of physical types as might be seen today strolling along the Arno River in Florence, working in the vineyards of Tuscany or crowding into one of the great cathedrals of Rome.

A World of Delights for the Affluent

"Moment . . . abide, you are so fair!" That cry of Goethe's bewitched Faust might well have been the motto of the Etruscans—at least those born to noble estate. Their exuberant gaiety, fed by a wide range of pastimes, is captured in the rich tomb frescoes that appear here and on the following pages. They banqueted with gusto, cultivated dancing, and delighted in hunting, fishing, making love and engaging in rigorous, competitive sport.

Musicians were often present when the people of Etruria pleasured themselves. The tunes were usually played on the double pipe (right), an instrument best described as a pair of conjoined oboes, with holes to be covered by the fingers of each hand. The double pipe was suited to the tonal systems most popular among Etruscans: the Phrygian, Hypophrygian, Lydian and Hypolydian—defined respectively by Classical music theorists, according to mood, as agitated, active, melancholic and voluptuous.

A gracefully clad piper dances to his own music in this scene from the Tomb of the Triclinium at Tarquinii, painted around 470 B.C. His hair is short, the fashion current at the time, and he wears only a brief gossamer cloak.

Dalliance and Good Talk at Dinner

The Etruscans appalled their more inhibited neighbors, the Greeks and Romans, with their habit of feasting twice a day, consuming delicacies ranging from turtle eggs to wild boar. Yet they were not gluttons; they reclined at mealtime for entertainment, conversation and—if company was present—flirtation. Indeed, the banqueting couples in many instances seem much more absorbed in each other than in the food; the man and woman in the fresco at top right are paying no attention to the musician and servants attending them. In other paintings the mood is playful, as with the dashing pairs at bottom right, served by two nude attendants. The lively scene might have been a picnic, a possibility suggested by the trees in the background.

In this Sixth Century B.C. painting from the Tomb of the Lionesses, a pensive banqueter holds up an egg, symbol of life's continuity—in his case, a good life. The man's massive proportions, which dwarf the figure on the next wall, indicate he is an important relative of the deceased.

Dining among garlands woven by the servants at left, a wife gazes at her husband in a 520 B.C. fresco from the Tomb of Hunting and Fishing.

Three carefree couples, all crowned with myrtle, enjoy a dinner in this festive scene, painted around 480 B.C. in the Tomb of the Leopards.

"Movements Not Without Grace"

Dancing was in every Etruscan's blood. Tomb paintings catch warriors, musicians, servants, aristocrats and professional dancers in midstep, executing motions that may have been religious or orgiastic, or just a physical reaction to a tune and a beat. There was, however, some method to the general abandon; professional performers, at least, followed strict patterns. A Roman writer, in a patronizing mood, spoke of Etruscans as capable of "performing movements not without grace"; one of their routines may have involved stamping their feet on the ground three times and then projecting themselves in a series of leaps. The artists who created the frescoes placed great emphasis on the attitudes of the fingers and positions of the hands.

A dancing girl twirls to the music of a piper (right) and the hand clapping of a man wearing a bearded mask in a painting in the Tomb of the Rooster, rendered in the Fourth Century B.C. The girl holds elongated wooden castanets, which she clicks to echo the rhythm marked by the hand clapper.

Arching her booted right leg, a young woman bends her slender hands in conformity with a prescribed dance routine. The painting, found in the Tomb of the Jugglers and done in the Sixth Century B.C., appears to be a portrait, a scholarly judgment based on her distinctive appearance: strong profile, large eyes and dark hair.

This frenetic, sensuous dance from The Tomb of the Lionesses resembles a freewheeling modern ballet. The youth holds a wine jug; his flimsily clad partner holds her hand in a gesture that suggests the horns of a bull or the sign for a cuckold.

Joyous Pastimes at the Shore

Only five miles from the sea, Tarquinii offered its inhabitants all the natural pleasures of a maritime resort. The paintings on these pages, from the Sixth Century B.C. Tomb of Hunting and Fishing, conjure up a typical day at the shore: men fish, hunt birds, scramble up cliffs and dive into the water. The Etruscans loved nature. They hunted frequently and with relish. Classical writings confirm that there was even a game preserve near Tarquinii, whose owner raised hares, deer and wild sheep for the chase. Animals appear constantly in Etruscan frescoes: as game, as pets or simply as decorative motifs. The focal characters in the wall paintings of this tomb are not the humans, but graceful birds and a dolphin gaily turning a somersault, such as those in the picture opposite.

A youth dives from a boulder into the sea far below. His companion raises a hand—suggesting that the diver may have been playfully pushed and forced to make the best of the fall.

In this lively tableau, a hunter on a cliff fires slingshots flock of birds while two of his companions in the boat b cheer him on. The undistracted fisherman lowers his lin while an oarsman steers. The great eye painted on the p probably was a traditional emblem to help guide the boo

Sports contests were not only a leisure pastime for the people of Etruria but also a central aspect of religious festivals. The determined sportsmen in this fresco from the Tomb of the Olympiads, painted in the Sixth Century B.C., confirm the Etruscans' early addiction to track and field events, a passion they shared with the Greeks. The figures at left below are obviously involved in a foot race. The man in the center is flexing his arms preparatory to a jump. At right, a discus thrower sets himself. In painting the athletes, the artist has brilliantly conveyed a sense of effort and muscular tension.

For all their love of the high life and their sensuous appreciation of it, Etruscans were a religion-ridden people, the most god-fearing of their times. In the absence of clarifying evidence, the relationship between the two apparently contradictory attitudes is puzzling; but the Etruscans certainly believed that the pleasures of life on earth could continue after death, and so they may have felt it essential that the living gain the good will of the gods in order to guarantee an enjoyable afterlife.

The only known original Etruscan sacred text of any length is the Linen Book, found wrapped around the Zagreb mummy *(page 40)*—a work that still defies full understanding. But there is ample other evidence of an obsessive preoccupation with religion —in tomb paintings, in the remains of temples and shrines, in inscriptions on funerary monuments and on pots, figurines and other objects that served as votive offerings. Even more revealing are the writings of contemporary Romans who observed Etruscan religion as it was practiced, or who had access to Etruscan holy books, now vanished, which they translated into Latin; Livy, for example, said that the Etruscans were "more concerned than any other nation with religious matters." Some of these Latin translations still exist, if only in fragments. Although the Romans may sometimes have misinterpreted what they saw or read, they were beyond question as-

With the aid of two winged goddesses, the principal Etruscan deity, Tinia, gives birth—from the crown of his head—to the goddess of wisdom, Menrva, in this engraving on the back of a Fourth Century B.C. bronze mirror, which is seven inches in diameter. Although Tinia was revered as the supreme deity, he often had to seek the consent of other gods and to report, as well, to a council of omniscient and superior authorities.

tounded by the time and effort the Etruscans devoted to religious pursuits, by the enormous number of their gods and by the extent of the hierarchies into which those gods were arranged.

Not a few of the deities making up this pantheon, while apparently of legitimate Etruscan origin, were strongly influenced by the divinities of ancient Greece. By the early Sixth Century B.C. these gods more or less paralleled their Greek models in appearance and, in many cases, in function as well. For example, the important Etruscan gods Tinia, Uni and Menrva had their close counterparts in the Greeks' Zeus, Hera and Athena; in turn, these deities had their counterparts in the Romans' Jupiter, Juno and Minerva. The Etruscans had also borrowed some gods directly from the Greeks—among them Apollo, called Aplu by the Etruscans, and Artemis, known as Aritimi in Etruria. In addition to the major Etruscan deities—at least a dozen in number—there were scores of other gods who acted as their helpers or counselors, as well as swarms of local gods and supernatural beings.

Judged by the divine rosters of other ancient religions, the Etruscans were not unusual in worshiping a multitude of divinities. But the intensity of their belief was peculiarly their own. The people of Etruria held that man was powerless in the face of the capricious gods, and the Etruscans believed in the necessity of divining and obeying the gods' wishes—or placating them—through complex and rigidly observed rituals.

Elements of human helplessness, of god-searching, permeate all religions, but the abjectness of highborn Etruscans in the face of their deities was in marked contrast to the attitudes of their Greek and Roman contemporaries. Greek philosophers tempered their religious beliefs with logic, and the Romans with hard-eyed practical considerations (though the simple folk of both peoples did hold many superstitions and were devoted to miracle-working sanctuaries and magic practices).

The Romans subjected their religion to close examination—as if they had contracts with the gods and the fine print included possible loopholes. For instance, the Romans believed it was disastrous for yoked animals to defecate simultaneously while approaching the shrine where they were to be sacrificed. To avoid such a possibility of angering a god, they simply unyoked the beasts at a safe distance from the shrine. In such fashion the letter of religious law was respected, but its spirit was frequently circumvented.

Not so in Etruria. There the people believed that the working out of the simplest, most common, most predictable events in the lives of men, of animals, of plants—birth and growth and death—was decreed and preordained. As Seneca, the First Century A.D. Roman philosopher, described the Etruscan faith: "The difference between us and the Etruscans . . . is the following: that whereas we believe lightning to be released as a result of the collision of clouds, they believe that clouds collide so as to release lightning. For as they attribute all to the deity, they believe not that things have a meaning in so far as they occur, but rather that they happen because they must have a meaning."

Thus Etruscans had a single overwhelming need: to discover the meanings behind occurrences and to read from them the messages and wishes of the gods. The attempt to do so led to the emergence of a huge, powerful priestly class of soothsayers drawn from the aristocracy. The elite of this group were called in Etruscan *netsvis* or *trutnvt frontac*, but are more familiarly known as *haruspices* and *fulguriatores* —their Latin designations. *Haruspices* had the ability to read omens in the entrails of sacrificed animals, particularly the liver; *fulguriatores* could interpret divine will by studying thunder and lightning. (Occasionally the functions of lightning reader and entrails reader were combined in one person; an epitaph in Latin from a late Etruscan tomb, found at Pesaro on the Adriatic Sea, describes a man who was adept at reading omens through both techniques.)

Haruspices and *fulguriatores* based their divination on a complex, mystical-magical division of the universe that was unique to Etruria. Many other ancient religions—among them the Babylonian, the Hebrew of Old Testament days and early Christianity —saw the universe as divided into quarters determined by the four cardinal points of the compass. But the Etruscans went much further and subdivided the four quarters into a total of 16 sectors, in which their gods resided. A detailed diagram of this peculiarly Etruscan universe is engraved on a bronze representation of a liver found in 1877 in the northern Italian city of Piacenza, southeast of Milan; the artifact is believed to have been a teaching device for training *haruspices*.

Each segment of the Etruscan universe was identified with a chief god, who had a specific area of influence—the heavens, the earth and nature, fate, and so forth—but because of the lack of original Etruscan documents and possible misinterpretations by Roman writers, the gods who reigned in some segments are obscure.

Text continued on page 92

Sheltering Urns for Transient Souls

Etruscans were fearful of the passage from this world to the next, and believed that the spirit of a person recently dead was in peril of a horrible transformation. To provide lodgings for the souls of the deceased and to safeguard the ashes of cremated bodies, the Etruscans commissioned potters, sculptors and smiths to produce urns that were partly or wholly anthropomorphic. Besides preserving homeless spirits from harm, the receptacles may also have given the ghost a human shape for its existence beyond the grave.

Pierced with holes that may have held a mask in place, a brooding seven-inch-high terra-cotta head forms the top of a funerary urn.

A Free Mix of Shapes and Styles

The four Etruscan funerary vessels on these pages—all from the same vicinity in Tuscany, all made during the Sixth Century B.C.—vary in size, style and material. They range from cartoon-like abstractions to what appear to be portraits of the person whose ashes they held. Part of this diversity, scholars speculate, reflected the social positions of the people who commissioned them; the rich could afford more elaborate provisions for death than could the less affluent. Despite the artistic variety with which the heads were treated, until late in the century the lower portions of the receptacles were never fashioned into fully human form.

On the lid of a 35-inch urn, a female figure in terra cotta presses her left arm against her breast in supplication; birdlike guardians and tiny human mourners surround her.

This stylized 17-inch-high terra-cotta vessel only partly represents a human. The lid is shaped like a woman's head, but the body is merely a jar with hands and breasts.

A realistic terra-cotta head becomes a surrealistic top for a bronze ash container, which though nonhuman in form sits on a terra-cotta throne. The urn stands 24 inches high overall.

A 54-inch figure of a seated man carved in limestone is the most lifelike of the urns yet found. The painted eyes and expressive hands suggest a carefully wrought portrait.

It is clear, however, that Tinia ruled in the northeastern segments and that he was the most powerful god in the Etruscan pantheon—a hurler of thunderbolts like his Greek and Roman equivalents, Zeus and Jupiter. His dominion extended over three sections, in parts of which he shared power with his wife Uni.

Also in these northeastern sectors were assistant and advisory gods and lesser deities, all of them puzzling even to the Romans and very dimly understood today. The most important were those the Romans sometimes described as the *Dii Superiores*, the Supreme Gods. They apparently acted as a high court or council of ministers, offering advice and counsel to Tinia and other high-ranking deities. Tinia also consulted with about a dozen *Dii Consentes*, or Consenting Gods, and an unknown number of *Dii Involuti*, or Involved Gods, whose chief function seems to have been to advise Tinia on when and where to hurl his thunderbolts toward earth.

Moving clockwise around the compass of the universe, the northeast areas dominated by Tinia and his wife, Uni, were followed by eastern regions under the sway of Menrva, goddess of wisdom and the arts, Belchans, the god of fire, and Turms, the Etruscan version of the Greek messenger god Hermes and of the Roman Mercury. At the south lay the domain of Catha, the sun god; and nearby, that of Fufluns, a wine god similar to the Greek Dionysus or the Roman Bacchus. In the northwest lay the sectors dominated by the gods of the underworld and of misfortune. In almost all ancient religions, the west was identified with the fear of death—perhaps because it was where the sun set, ending the day's life. (The identification of death with the west has persisted; as late as World War I, fallen English and American

Flanked by two shepherds, the head of the mythical child-prophet Tages emerges from the ground. This impression was made from a gem stone half an inch long that was incised in the late Second Century B.C. According to legend, Tages' gray head appeared one day in a newly plowed field, chanted to its awe-struck listeners the doctrine from which all Etruscan divine wisdom flowed and then sank down again.

soldiers were referred to as having "gone west.")

Once they had delineated the regions of the universe and had established the heavenly order, the Etruscans concerned themselves with the matter of orientation—the direction from which celestial influences were projected down to earth. Scholars have concluded that the Etruscans, uniquely, faced south when contemplating the heavens. In contrast, the Greeks and Romans viewed the universe with their backs to the south and their faces to the north, and thus considered right lucky, left unlucky. The Latin word for left is *sinister*.

The matter of orientation was particularly important to the Etruscan soothsayers—the *fulguriatores* —whose specialty was reading the portents in thunder and lightning. Facing south, the soothsayer carefully determined whether the lightning bolts came from left or right; the precise point of departure of the lightning and thunder from the heavens indicated exactly which gods had loosed them. In addition to the chief god Tinia, who could throw his thunderbolts from any part of his heavenly domain, eight other gods in the Etruscan hierarchy had the right to hurl lightning. They included Uni, Menrva, Maris (who had his counterpart in the Roman war god Mars) and a god of agriculture resembling the Roman Saturn. Thus there were 11 different directions from which benign or disastrous natural fireworks could come.

Under the elaborate ground rules, however, only Tinia's thunderbolts were to be dreaded. His bolts were of three types; his first, hurled whenever he wished, was in the nature of an alert. But before he could throw another, he had to ask the *Dii Consentes*. This second bolt was generally of good omen. Then,

Tinia could hurl a third only if he first obtained permission from both the *Dii Superiores* and the *Dii Involuti,* and its effect could be Armageddon: kings struck dead, armies confused on the battlefield, crops destroyed, flood and famine.

To assist them in their work the *fulguriatores* drew up elaborate time charts, known today as brontoscopic calendars. (Traces of the ancient awe and fear of celestial events lie in a modern scientific term that is occasionally heard in everyday Italian: *brontofobia,* a fear of thunder.)

Fragments of one such calendar that had been translated into Latin—and that later was translated from Latin into Greek by a Byzantine writer—were found by a French scholar and published in 1951. This astonishing document reveals the detailed state of the *fulguriatores'* art. Potential misfortunes specifically foreseen by the soothsayers were assigned to precise dates. For example, thunder on a date corresponding to September 11 indicated that *eteras*—dependents of the nobility who performed special and valued services—would instigate a political revolution against their patrons. A loud clap on October 24 meant that tensions between peasants and rulers would lead to the overthrow of the masters. If it thundered on December 3, fishermen would find their nets empty and the people would have to slaughter domestic animals for food. A bolt on July 14 indicated that power would pass to the hands of one man, who would misuse it.

Even more exotic to the modern mind than *fulguriatores* are the *haruspices,* or entrails readers. Etruscans considered the liver the seat of life, a quivering internal organic representation of the celestial universe. Just why the Etruscans hit upon the liver is not clear; possibly they got the idea from Eastern peo-

Reading Heavenly Portents

To Etruscans, second-guessing the desires and intentions of their many gods was vital. Soothsayers, therefore, devised elaborate means of divining the gods' moods. One method consisted of reading the entrails—particularly the livers—of animals. This form of augury was based on the belief that the liver reflected the organization of the universe *(far right)*, and that its parts corresponded to the provinces ruled by different deities. Diviners looked for telltale spasms or lumps in the extracted organ of a sacrificed animal to determine which gods were at work and what to hope for—or fear—from them.

A winged and bearded mythical diviner peers over a sheep's liver in this scene on a bronze mirror from the Fifth Century B.C. Although not wearing an augur's traditional clothes (page 97), the sage holds the proper ritual stance: liver in left hand, left arm on left knee and left foot resting on a boulder.

Found near the town of Piacenza, this bronze model of a sheep's liver was probably used to teach diviners their trade around the Third Century B.C. The 16 names engraved on the liver's edge match the 16 parts of the Etruscan universe. The names of minor gods cover the liver's center and one of the upright protuberances, which represent adjacent organs.

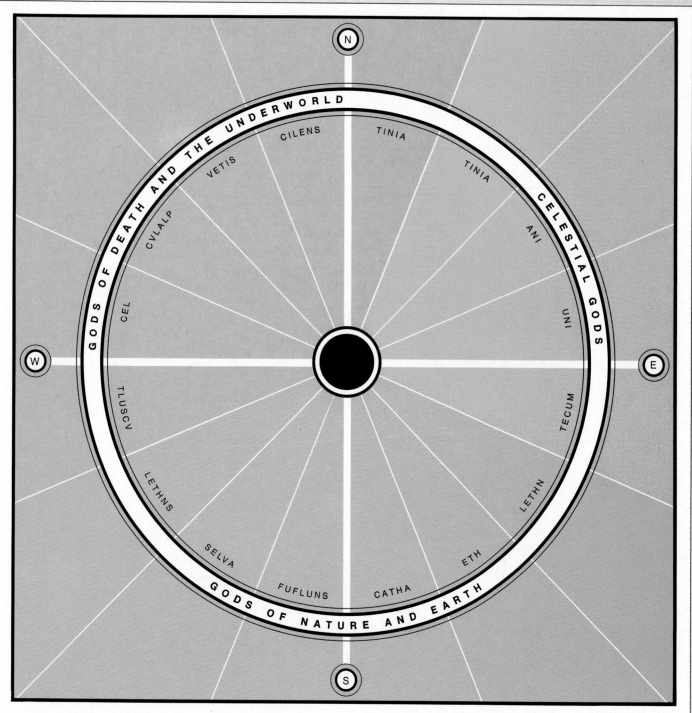

Based on Roman accounts, the chart above illustrates in simplified form the Etruscan concept of a cosmos in which three major forces operated: heavenly (orange), earthly (green) and underworldly (blue). The 16 subdivisions of this realm were dominated by 15 major gods; Tinia, the chief deity, held sway over two sectors, and thus he was both a god of death and the underworld and a celestial god. Man's place was at the center; he faced south, where the gods of nature and earth dwelled. The west lay to his right and the east to his left. Since dark forces ruled the west and benevolent ones the east, the Etruscans deemed the right unlucky and the left fortuitous. Pervading all Etruscan belief, this division of the universe was used not only in divination but also in the planning of cities and in the placement of temples.

ples who endowed the liver with special importance. Divinations from this organ first appeared in human history about 2000 B.C. in Babylonia, and occur until about 1200 B.C. in the Hittite Empire of Asia Minor, but no clear links have yet been found that would have carried the practice across the centuries to Etruscan times.

Just how the *haruspices* read a liver after it had been snatched, steaming, from the body of a sacrificial animal, is obscure. Visual examination may have sufficed, but the sense of touch—how the liver felt to the reader's trained fingers—may also have been important. Whatever the method, Etruscan *haruspices* could use the readings to advise their people either to alter their conduct or to appease the appropriate gods by special ceremonial dances, music and votive offerings at altars.

The Etruscan manner of divination was accepted as eminently efficacious, not only in Etruria but also in Rome. An especially well-documented case of the Romans' calling upon the soothsayers of Etruria was reported by the august statesman and orator Cicero. In 56 B.C. strange rumblings were heard by many residents in one sector of the city. It was a time of civic turmoil, when republican Rome was governed by a quarreling triumvirate and both nobles and ordinary citizens—plebeians—were beset by warring street gangs paid by powerful citizens. *Haruspices* summoned from Etruria studied the ominous noises, read the omens and made a meticulous diagnosis: the disturbance was being caused by the Etruscan equivalents of the gods Jupiter, Saturn, Neptune and Tellurus, the earth god. The reason for the divine anger was clear, the *haruspices* said: men had neglected their religious duties, had paid no attention to their sacred oaths and had murdered orators—a sacrilege since orators were symbols of social order.

Cicero himself had barely escaped murder at the hands of a relative and neighbor who, for political reasons, had become his sworn enemy. Cicero thought that the worst of the rumbling came from the nearby house of that enemy; the neighbor believed, in turn, that the noise originated from Cicero's house. The Etruscan *haruspices*—whose names Cicero did not record—were, at least, not fools; they refrained from taking sides. They contented themselves diplomatically with warning the Romans to beware of discord between arrogant nobles and discontented plebeians, and to be alert to plots that might cause the downfall of the regime.

That cautious interpretation must have been too pat to support the *haruspices'* reputation as diviners of things to come. Certainly, upper-class Romans of 56 B.C. had had ample experience of such plots, and it was abundantly obvious that nobles and plebeians were constantly at each other's throats. Perhaps because of carefully qualified predictions, both Greek and Roman intellectuals of the period had grown outspokenly skeptical of the art of divination.

Nevertheless, the common folk still accepted a *haruspex's* word as gospel. And many influential Romans continued a long-standing custom of retaining Etruscan soothsayers as advisors—just in case. The noble Gracchi brothers, statesmen and social reformers of the Second Century B.C., retained a personal *haruspex* with the Latinized name of Herennius Siculus. And it was Julius Caesar's personal Etruscan *haruspex*, Spurinna, who warned him—in vain—to "beware the ides of March" in 44 B.C. During the ides, Caesar was murdered.

Though highly stylized, these foot-long bronze figurines, from about the Third Century B.C., accurately show the ritual garb of an Etruscan holy man: a cloak fastened with a brooch and a high conical hat. Each priest holds a sacrificial cup in his right hand; his left hand makes a gesture of worship.

The great Etruscan soothsayers came on center stage for the last time long after the glory of Etruria itself had faded. Early in the Fifth Century A.D., in a curious reversion to paganism—perhaps invoked to pander to the superstition of the always restive Roman populace—Pope Innocent I consulted both *haruspices* and *fulguriatores* in the defense of the Holy See. The Pope asked the soothsayers to direct thunderbolts upon an invading army of Visigoths under the leadership of Alaric. The desperate measure failed, and Rome was sacked.

To Etruscans of an earlier era, the failure would have been easy to explain: insufficient faith. In Etruscan tradition, unquestioning belief in all the precepts —in the intricate plan of the universe, in the organization of celestial powers, in the art of divination itself and in the proper forms of rituals—was indispensable to successful soothsaying. Belief and religious practice were both firmly based on the instructions of sages who had appeared miraculously to unlock sacred secrets to human beings.

The rules of their religion first came to the Etruscans from two legendary figures. The first and most important, called Tages, appeared near Tarquinii, the first Etruscan city to rise to power. One day, the story goes, a farmer's plow cut a furrow deeper than usual. From the furrow emerged a being who is sometimes represented with the innocent, unformed aspect of a human baby, sometimes with the body of a baby and the wrinkled face and white hair of an elder. This young-old figure introduced himself to the farmer and his astonished neighbors as Tages, and proceeded to explain to the local elders the secrets of the universe and the gods, and the basic elements of soothsaying.

Etruscans also venerated a nymphlike figure called Vegoia, or Begoe, who imparted her wisdom to a human named Arruns, apparently a king or priest of the city of Clusium. A fragment of her teachings still exists in a Latin translation. Although amended by an unidentified *haruspex* for the particular purpose of rallying the Etruscans during troubled times in the First Century B.C., the document embodies principles laid down long before by the gods and relayed through Vegoia. It reads, in part:

"Know that the sea was separated from the sky. Now, when Jupiter had claimed back the land of Etruria"—from whom or from what is not explained—"he established and commanded that the plains should be surveyed and the fields limited. Knowing well that human avarice and passion is excited by land, he desired that everything should be defined by boundary-marks. One day, when moved by avarice, someone will treat these bounds with contempt; men, by fraudulent means, will lay hands upon them or displace them. But whosoever shall touch and displace them in order to extend his property and diminish that of others shall for this crime be condemned by the gods. Then shall the earth often be shaken by tempests and whirlwinds that will make it tremble."

Though the first sentence sounds like the Biblical Book of Genesis in its sweeping evocation of creation and the separation of sea from sky, the rest of the passage focuses on the Etruscans' concept of the sacred, inviolable nature of boundaries and property rights. The roots of this attitude must reach far back to the very origins of Etruscan belief, but in this case the warning tone of Vegoia's message was a reflection of immediate stresses and was circulated as propaganda. When this extract appeared in 91 B.C.,

Roman land reforms were threatening to break up Etruscan holdings, and the establishment of Roman colonies in areas formerly controlled by Etruscans further weakened their control over the fields they loved and considered their own.

The wisdom of Vegoia and Tages was collected, edited, amended and, along with other religious texts, incorporated into a corpus of holy books that made up the bulk of Etruscan literature. The books themselves no longer exist except for fragments—of which the inscription wrapped around the Zagreb mummy is the longest—but they were well known and respected in the Roman world. The Romans, in translating at least some of them, collectively named the books *Etrusca Disciplina.*

There were three fundamental parts of the *Etrusca Disciplina,* known respectively to the Romans as the *Libri Haruspicini,* the *Libri Fulgurales* and the *Libri Rituales.* The first group of books, as the name implies, dealt with divination from animal entrails; the second, with the interpretation of lightning; the third group covered a wide-ranging list of rules and rituals, involving such formalities as worship, the consecration of sanctuaries, the founding of cities and the division of lands.

There were also special sections on the understanding of miracles, on destiny and the time allotted to the lives of men and nations, on funerary rituals and life in the hereafter. These codes of rules and principles were assembled as the *Libri Acherontici* —deriving its name from the Acheron, one of several mythological rivers that, along with the Styx, formed the boundaries of the Greek underworld.

The Romans' respect for the teachings of the *Etrusca Disciplina* is markedly evident in the fact that one of their most important rituals was adopted from an Etruscan custom prescribed in the *Libri Rituales:* the solemn ceremony of city founding and planning. Their tradition held that Rome itself had been founded according to the Etruscan ritual and, as the city's power grew, the ceremony was rigidly adhered to in establishing new towns and cities throughout the Italian peninsula and in the provinces abroad. To the Roman mind, the ultimate praise that could be bestowed upon a city was to say that it had been founded in the *more Etrusco*—the Etruscan manner.

To the Etruscans, city-founding ceremonies were too important to be entrusted to anyone but their high priests. The seers read the signs and portents, laid out the crucial boundaries on auspicious days and then supervised the ritual that marked the perimeter of the new city. A white bull and cow, yoked together, pulled a bronze-bladed plow, and as it dug a furrow to trace the boundaries, eager hands placed all the clods of plowed earth on the side of the furrow toward the city-to-be.

At the future center of the city, workmen dug a trench into which the founding fathers tossed a handful of earth from their native home. Then the trench was covered with a vault of stone. From the city center, the priest laid out the main thoroughfare and calculated the course of the principal cross street. The Etruscan term for the central trench is unknown —the Romans called it the *mundus*—and its significance to the Etruscans is not clear. To them, it may have represented something more than the physical heart of the city. Perhaps they visualized it as the Romans did: a meeting point for the world of the living and the dead. On very holy occasions, such as the anniversary of a city's founding, the Romans custom-arily opened the vault of the *mundus* to offer fruit and other gifts to the spirits of the underworld; the ceremony was one means of placating the supernatural agents of evil fortune.

While some rituals, like those associated with city founding, have come down to modern scholarship either because the Romans adopted them or described them in their writings, little is known about how the Etruscans worshipped within their temples. In earliest times the Etruscans had performed their rites of worship in the open, upon simple stone or earthen platforms raised in sacred areas. Actual temples —buildings with roofs and enclosed sanctuaries—did not appear until the late Sixth Century B.C. Precisely how these temples looked is not known. Except for their stone foundations, Etruscan temples, like Etruscan houses, were built of perishable wood and mud brick and terra cotta, a fragile material; thus their ruins do not stand forth boldly like those of many Greek and Roman sanctuaries made almost entirely of stone. Archeologists have uncovered a few foundations to indicate layout, some roof tiles, fragments of decorative friezes and the remains of stone altars. But such traces, supplemented by temple models found in tombs and the temple-like façades of some of the sanctuaries themselves, are sufficient to show that Etruscan shrines from about the Fourth Century B.C. onward could be elaborate structures with columned porticoes, pediments adorned with handsome terra-cotta bas-reliefs and peaked roofs surmounted by freestanding single or grouped figures sculptured in the same material.

For many years scholars thought that all Etruscan temples were built facing south so that their priests could keep the most auspicious segment of the heavens—the northeast—on their left side. Scholars also accepted the word of the Roman architect and engineer Vitruvius, who wrote in the First Century B.C. that Etruscan temples consisted of three rooms, or cellae, dedicated to the principal Etruscan deities Tinia, Uni and Menrva.

Both ideas have been revised in the wake of recent archeological excavations. For example, diggers at Murlo, a site south of Siena, turned up a temple with a single cella that was oriented not to the south but —logically enough—to the northeast. At Graviscae, near the Etruscan city of Tarquinii, a temple with two cellae has come to light. It seems clear, therefore, that there was no single, rigid pattern for temple design and orientation.

Given the apparent Etruscan devotion to precise rules and procedures for their sacred rites, that absence of pattern is odd. Equally strange is the fact that the temples, focal points of the religion that dominated every aspect of Etruscan life, did not consist of more enduring materials. Stone was readily available. Most of it was soft tufa, but the Etruscans certainly knew how to quarry harder stone and to dress it into blocks for building structures like city walls. In some places they laboriously carved their cemeteries in basalt and limestone, the hardest stone they could find.

The reason they did not use tough and lasting materials for their temples may lie in the Etruscan hope of a happy posthumous existence. The Etruscan mind made a distinction between the struggles of the living and the peaceful prospect of eternal afterlife enjoyed by the dead. Perhaps they considered the temple a temporary structure—created to enhance the influence of religion on a transitory earthly life, a place in which to adjust the accounts between gods and living men or between men and their neighbors. In contrast, the tomb, set apart from these turbulent affairs, would have had to be an indestructible stone home, deep in the earth, where human problems were shut out forever.

There is no question that the Etruscans were fatalists, with a clear-eyed vision of their own temporal mortality. Even so, through most of their history theirs was a fatalism not unmixed with optimism. According to the sacred writings in their *Libri Rituales,* they hopefully assigned to man a maximum life span that seems to have been 12 times seven years—a concept totally at odds with their actual experience; analyses of skeletal remains indicate that an Etruscan's life expectancy actually hovered around 40 years. They also allotted a maximum span for the power of Etruria itself. The soothsayers had told them that their preeminence would last 10 *saecula* —that is, 10 Etruscan centuries. Just how long an Etruscan *saeculum* was, no one knows; scholars estimate that it may have been as few as 80 and as many as 120 years. In that prediction, too, the Etruscans were poignantly—and mistakenly—optimistic.

Lively Sculptures from Vanished Temples

Although Etruscan artists did not make images of their own remote and faceless deities, the Greek pantheon—incorporated into Etruscan religious life after the Seventh Century B.C.—provided them with a rich new array of divine subject matter. In the Sixth Century B.C., Etruscan sculptors avidly set to work portraying Greek gods and sprites and their exploits. Indeed, in the heyday of Etruscan temple building, from the Sixth to the Fourth Century B.C., Etruria's sanctuaries were so crowded with figures that Greeks, used to modest decoration, disapproved of the extravagant displays.

Painted terra cotta was the only material used for temple statues and decorations. Pliny the Elder, a First Century A.D. Roman historian, commended the brilliant use of pottery when he wrote of the "many temples whose roofs are still adorned with terra-cotta figures, remarkable for their modeling and artistic quality as well as their durability [that are] more deserving of respect than gold."

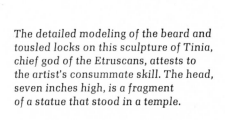

The detailed modeling of the beard and tousled locks on this sculpture of Tinia, chief god of the Etruscans, attests to the artist's consummate skill. The head, seven inches high, is a fragment of a statue that stood in a temple.

Divinities for Sanctuary Roofs

Because the Etruscans seem to have regarded stone suitable mainly for honoring the dead, they built their temples of sun-dried brick and wood—materials that perish with time. Nevertheless, experts have gained a fairly clear idea of how a typical Etruscan temple looked from cinerary urns shaped like tiny shrines and, more importantly, from the writings of the architect Vitruvius, who lived in Rome late in the First Century B.C. He had seen a number of late Etruscan shrines, but rather than record the exact dimensions of each, he made up a canon of the proportions and structure of an ideal Etruscan temple. As a rule, Vitruvius stated, the length of the rectangular temple was divided equally between an enclosed sanctuary and an eight-columned porch. It was set on a high platform approached by a steep flight of steps. The figures that embellished the roof were so firmly fitted into settings on the tiles that they could remain upright through the ravages of storm, wind and time.

This three-foot-wide model of a Sixth Century B.C. Etruscan temple built at Rome University was made according to the proportions and specifications set down by the Roman architect Vitruvius. All the large statues and small decorations were copied from finds at Veii associated with the Portonaccio temple. The roof was adorned with statuary. A Fourth Century B.C. model would show the triangular pediment, or gable, filled with more figures, as were the temple's eaves on the front and the sides.

This powerfully built, striding Apollo—known to the Etruscans as Aplu—once stood upon the roof of the Portonaccio temple in Veii. His hair is dressed in a Greek style, but he wears the short Etruscan cloak and tunic. Discovered in 1916, the six-foot statue is believed to be a masterwork of the Sixth Century B.C. sculptor Vulca— the only Etruscan artist whose name has survived to today.

Also from the temple at Veii is this 13-inch head of Hermes, known to the Etruscans as Turms; the body has been lost. His slanting eyes and curved lips are in the archaic Greek style that the artists of Veii so admired.

Heroic Figures in Spirited Action

Etruscan artists excelled at making powerful figure groupings. Frequently the artists paid less attention to human anatomical proportions than they did to costume details and to such features as eyes, hair and beards. The figure of Menrva, far left in the group opposite, for instance, wears a tiered tunic that falls in flat folds. Her hair, and that of the Medusa on her breastplate, is tightly crimped. Etruscan artists were close observers of nature, however, and could sculpt figures of almost photographic realism, as evinced in the team of horses below. The manes of these elegant steeds seem blown by a wind—a touch that adds movement to the pair.

Matched stallions, 45 inches high, once drew a chariot across the pediment of a Third Century B.C. temple at Tarquinii. The blend of realism and fantasy—perfectly fitting harnesses contrasted with purely imaginary wings—is an Etruscan artistic trait.

The goddess Menrva at the far left observes a writhing foursome of deities and giants. Tinia strides in front of her, his body sharply twisted and his arm raised menacingly. Sprawled in the foreground, a god wrestles a giant to the ground. By contorting and overlapping the figures, the unknown artist compressed a scene of violent action into a relatively small space. The group, measuring five feet across, once filled the center of the pediment at the Fifth Century B.C. temple at Pyrgi.

A fragment 30 inches wide of two contesting warriors, one broken off at the hip, adorned a Sixth Century B.C. temple at Falerii Veteres. Exactly where the figures were placed is uncertain: they were either poised atop the temple's ridgepole or wedged into a corner of the pediment over the entrance.

A Gallery of Mythic Guardians

Antefixes—terra-cotta reliefs affixed to tiles and decorated with human or fantastic heads—covered and protected the wooden temple eaves. A Greek invention, antefixes were adopted by the Etruscans with their usual enthusiasm for Grecian art forms. Gods, demons and maenads—mortal women who participated in the mythical orgies of the wine god Dionysus—were the usual subjects, and were perfectly suited to the Etruscan love of color and variety. The artists' imaginations were given full rein to create images that ranged from the serene to the sinister. Antefixes not only served as practical coverings and as decorations, but they also were believed to be guardians against evil spirits. The tiles were made by itinerant potters who carried their molds from city to city. One mold could be used again and again. Clay was pressed into the molds; the clay was then fired and afterward it was gaudily painted.

The face of Achelous, a river god, wears a mischievous smile. In legend Achelous wrestled with the demigod Herakles disguised as a bull—hence the horn on his cap. This Fifth Century B.C. antefix is eight inches high.

The serene countenances of four lovely maenads flank a hideous Medusa. Though a fanlike edge—a Near Eastern art motif, representing a shell or a palmette—frames each face, the execution varies in style. The Medusa's mouth is stretched in a grin. Three maenads have knowing smiles and arching brows; but one, at the far right, wears a wistful expression. All five of these antefixes were made during the Fifth Century B.C. and range in height from less than 12 to almost 24 inches.

This five-inch head of Silenus, a satyr with the ears of a horse, has the swollen nose of the toper. The expression on the 11-inch visage of the maenad beside him seems demure by contrast. Both were made in the early Fifth Century B.C.

No amount of fatalism could have prepared the Etruscans for the series of disasters that overtook them in the Fourth Century B.C. Their shock as the blows began to fall is reflected in the paintings on their tomb walls and in the bas-reliefs decorating their sarcophagi. Where once all had been wine and dancing, music and laughter, there began to emerge, shortly after 400 B.C., an almost palpable aura of fear.

Etruscan art, once filled with happy scenes of banqueting or friendly spectator sports, now depicted bloody episodes borrowed largely from Greek legend and myth: the murder of Agamemnon, leader of the Greeks in the Trojan War, and of Clytemnestra, his faithless wife; the killing of Trojan captives in revenge for the slaying by Hector, the Trojan champion, of Patroclus, friend of the Greek hero Achilles; scenes of fratricide, human sacrifice and battles. Instead of pipe and lyre players there are hideous demons. Charun—whose name intimates his kinship to the Charon of Greek mythology, the god who ferried the dead across the river Styx—frequently appears beak-nosed and wild-eyed, clutching a hammer with which to dispatch those who fall into his hands and send them on to the next world. Charun has an equally unpleasant and purely Etruscan colleague, Tuchulcha, with the beak of a vulture, donkey's ears and horrid snakes wound about his head.

The crumbling of morale expressed by such gloomy

Representing the demon Charun, this garish seven-inch earthenware jug dates from the Fifth Century B.C. In Etruscan lore, Charun's function was to strike each mortal marked for death on the head, lead him to the underworld and there leave him to enjoy a happy afterlife. Charun became a common artistic subject as military defeats piled up and Etruscans felt forebodings of their political demise.

images had come about for two reasons. In the first place, there was a general decline in the business fortunes of Etruria. By the beginning of the Fourth Century B.C., the area of Etruscan commercial dominance had shrunk; the volume of trade—both at home and abroad—had receded. In addition the political life of the cities began to show signs of weakness as class conflicts between rulers and ruled became more and more exacerbated. Most important, the cities never had military cohesion and thus found themselves vulnerable to well-organized foes.

At no time was Etruria a nation, in the sense of having unity under a strong central government. Although the people shared a common language, religion and culture, they always lived in a loose collection of autonomous city-states much like those of ancient Greece.

The disparities among them were many, perpetuated by differences in their economies, cultural attitudes and environments. Each city had its own special source of wealth. Clusium and Perusia, for example, were in rich farming areas; Fufluna had its mining and smelting; Tarquinii and Vulci their flourishing metalcrafts. Caere, only a few miles from the Tyrrhenian coast, handled much of the trade between inland cities and the rest of the world.

Even the architecture varied from city to city, influenced by local tastes; and the layouts of the cities themselves differed according to the local terrain and whether they were founded from scratch by Etruscans or had gradually arisen on foundations laid down by others. In the older cities, often built on hills, the Etruscans may have made a special effort to give some order to the arrangement of temples and important public buildings, but the houses were

grouped more or less haphazardly on various levels and along streets that followed the terrain's winding contours, meandering up slope and down.

By contrast, other cities in less tortuous terrain and on virgin land, or on land that previously had not been heavily occupied, showed the benefit of deliberate planning. The ruins of such a city—the only one that has been fairly extensively excavated by archeologists—lie near the village of Marzabotto, south of Bologna. Probably called Misna or Misa by its Etruscan founders, it was established around 500 B.C. With a perimeter of nearly two and a half miles, it stood on generally level land in the valley of the Reno River. The area occupied by the homes of the inhabitants was a broad natural terrace divided by a main avenue almost 50 feet wide and running in a north-south direction. Intersecting this main thoroughfare at right angles were three major streets, each measuring about 17 feet across. The large rectangular city blocks formed by these principal arteries were further subdivided by a grid of lesser streets.

The leaders of the major city-states did meet once a year at a kind of pan-Etruscan festival; it was perhaps held at Volsinii, near Lake Bolsena in central Etruria, and was called the Fanum Voltumnae (page 116). Otherwise each city was a separate entity, dominating its adjacent territory and satellite settlements, but ceding power at the point where its territory impinged upon that of another city-state. The cities competed for trade and ascendancy; each established supremacy and then yielded it to successors. Such competition inevitably produced conflicts, though there is little evidence of the kind of bitter internecine warfare that destroyed the Greek city-states. On the other hand, Etruscan cities never joined all—or even most—of their forces against common peril.

Their shields and spears ready, the crewmen of a merchant ship prepare to stand off a Greek pirate galley. The battle scene appears on a Seventh Century B.C. terra-cotta vase 14 inches high. The massive sharp prow of the sailing craft may have been an Etruscan design meant to repel boarders.

The Fourth Century B.C. was rife with such challenges. Barbarian Gauls from across the Alps began to invade Etruscan lands north of the Po River early in the century, ultimately to descend on cities in central Etruria. Greek sea raiders from the colony of Syracuse launched hit-and-run attacks that struck Etruscan towns along the Adriatic and Tyrrhenian coasts as well as outposts on the islands of Corsica and Elba. But the most dangerous threat arose from an enemy close to home.

From the beginning of the century the politically disunited Etruscan cities increasingly found themselves pitted against the most formidable empire builders in history: the Romans. The fact that Etruscans had contributed enormously to the rise, the institutions and the customs of Rome did not save them. Neither did the fact that they had built many cities that were grander than Rome itself. The Roman legions swept forth, and in a series of bitter campaigns cut down Etruria's cities one by one.

Like all else about the Etruscans, the scenario of their rise and fall can be reconstructed in stages from the chronological sequence of their artifacts. When the Etruscans emerged into history around 750 B.C., and for more than a century thereafter, their cities were ruled by kings. Each wielded supreme political, judicial and religious power within his own domain. This ruler, called *lauchume* in Etruscan and *lucumo* in Latin, was accorded elaborate symbols of authority, among them the backless folding chair that survived into Roman times as the *sella curulis*, or magistrate's chair, and the bundle of rods surrounding an ax that became the Roman fasces.

The Etruscan fasces, representing the king's sovereignty, was carried by his attendants on ceremonial occasions; unlike the later Roman version, its central ax was double-bladed. (In republican Rome the consuls, or supreme authorities, who left the city as commanders of armies wielding the power of life and death, were accompanied by fasces, each fitted with a single-bladed ax. But when they were inside the city, the ax was removed, reflecting the fact that their power at home was limited.)

Roman tradition held that the first Etruscan city to use the fasces as a power symbol was Vetulonia—not far from the Tyrrhenian seacoast in present-day Tuscany. Indeed, the first specimen of an Etruscan fasces turned up in a cemetery at Vetulonia in the 1890s. The relic, dating from about 600 B.C., was a model made of iron and smaller than a real fasces would have been. It is exhibited today in the Florence Archeological Museum.

Whether or not kingship was hereditary in the early Etruscan city-states is not known. In Livy's history of Rome the first Tarquin ruler—an Etruscan —achieved the throne by election, and his successors were linked by lines of blood or marriage. Such bonds, however, were too weak to prevent matters of succession from being settled on occasion by recourse to assassination. A similar pattern—setting kinship and ambition into violent conflict—presumably prevailed in Italian cities other than Rome.

In any event, within two centuries after they entered the world scene, Etruscans began to replace their kings with ruling bodies whose member nobles were usually elected annually by their peers. This shift from monarchy to oligarchy also occurred in other contemporary societies around the Mediterranean, including those of the Phoenicians and the

A Fifth Century B.C. bas-relief from Clusium records a chariot race held to honor a dead dignitary. The limestone panel is a foot high.

Greeks. In each case the conversion probably came about spontaneously, as greater numbers of local aristocrats accumulated wealth and asserted more control over commerce and the religious establishment. As soon as they were strong enough, they moved to oust their monarchies and take power.

Most Etruscan cities seem to have made the switch to oligarchies by late in the Fifth Century B.C., although not all at the same time. Livy reports that the city of Veii, which had tried an oligarchy earlier, went back to a monarchy around 410 B.C. According to the Roman historian, the reconversion was made because Veii's citizens were disgusted "at the annually recurring scramble for office, which had not seldom given rise to bitter quarrels."

But for Etruscans in other cities who witnessed the restoration of the Veiian monarchy the reversion was repugnant—not only because the new king was unpopular personally, but because the reinstitution of his office struck a sour political note. Reading be-

tween the lines of Livy's account, a modern observer can draw a comparison between this response and the reaction of citizens in a modern democracy to the news that a neighboring country has been taken over by a dictatorship. Seen in this light, the anomalous Veiian experience has been viewed by some modern scholars as an indication that the other cities had expelled their monarchs and established oligarchies.

In time the oligarchies tended to become hereditary as a practical matter, though still theoretically elective; powerful families intermarried, passing their positions along to sons and other relatives, so that authority remained concentrated among a favored few. But the inheritance of power by a privileged handful inevitably weakened city governments by creating or aggravating tensions between the rulers and the ruled, making the cities vulnerable to internal revolt.

Occasionally this rigid division of society led to an actual breakdown of the oligarchy and eventually

The proud winner of a ritual combat, part of the funeral games opposite, is feted by a dancer and a piper as he reports his name to a scribe.

permitted the nonpatricians to win control by default. In such instances the interest of members of the ruling class in the business of governing had deteriorated; they were involved in the pursuit of pleasure and so delegated power to underlings, who took over such tasks as city administration. These functionaries may even have been allowed to carry arms. Before long the vital day-to-day operations of these cities fell firmly into the hands of such officials, whose taste of power gave them an appetite for full-fledged dominance. As a result the functionaries sometimes revolted, and the oligarchs had to call upon Rome for help in putting down the rebels.

One such emergency occurred in 265 B.C. in the city of Volsinii. According to some accounts, the Volsinian aristocrats had admitted a significant number of freed slaves to their own class both by intermarrying with them and by delegating to them authority for much of the city's management. Growing ever more ambitious, the former slaves rose up and tried

to take over supreme power. The Romans responded to the oligarchs' urgent appeal—but hardly as the rulers must have hoped they would. The Romans, who by that time already had humbled most of Etruria's cities, not only put down the rebellion but went on to destroy Volsinii itself.

The Romans did not need a pretext to bring down any Etruscan city; they had grown powerful enough to do so at whim. But their path of conquest probably would have been a great deal rougher had the rulers of Etruria's cities joined to fight together. The Greek historian Dionysius of Halicarnassus wrote of one occasion when the Etruscans did make a joint declaration of war against Rome, but there is no evidence that they followed through effectively. Livy reported at least two similar instances, although how united the actions might have been is unknown.

No satisfactory explanation has ever been proffered for this failure to make alliances. Again, the best guess is that the refusal to face up to hard real-

As if lost in some private sorrow, a man stares past his wife, who caresses his shoulder in a Third Century B.C. fresco from the Tomb of the Shields. As in the joyous painting on page 78, the egg he takes from her hand is a hopeful symbol of life. But despite their affluence—the couple can afford a servant (left) merely to fan them—their sad expressions dramatize the pessimism of the Etruscans in their decline.

ities was a consequence of the increasing effeteness of the Etruscan nobility—and a dwindling interest in the martial arts. Certainly, the Etruscans were aware of the advantages of unified action. It hardly seems possible they were blind to the fact that the Romans' triumphs stemmed precisely from their military discipline and organizational ability. Also they had the example of other populations in Italy that were capable of making effective common cause.

As one instance, the Samnites, who inhabited the central Apennines, were an amalgam of interrelated tribes sharing the same language, but linked mainly by geographical proximity. In the Fifth Century B.C. they combined to capture the southernmost major Etruscan city, on the site of modern Capua, and to expel the Etruscans from the region of Campania; and a century or so later the Samnites, with the strength born of their unity, were able to mount a serious threat to Rome itself—at least for a time.

Looking back to the period before the fragmentation of their society had escalated to the point of virtually destroying it, the people of Etruria must have known an excruciating despair as their towns and fields began to go down before Roman arms. Particularly bitter must have been the memory that Etruscan kings once had ruled Rome. In those days the city had been a strategic key to control of the south, a threat to Greek colonies and to any of the strong, independent tribes below Rome that might exhibit pretensions of power. But after the Romans expelled the last of their Etruscan kings, around 510 B.C., they set about making allies of or containing other current or potential foes. Within a century Roman strength had become a weapon pointed in the op-

posite direction. The fast-growing city turned toward its most powerful rival in the north: Etruria.

To be sure, the Etruscans, in loose alliances, had joined before to face formidable foes. Most of the time they had been victorious—but not always. In 474 B.C. they had lost a crucial naval battle to a Greek fleet from Syracuse off the Greek colony of Cumae, near present-day Naples. The defeat blocked further expansion deep into southern Italy. A half century later, when the Samnites swept out of their strongholds in the Apennines to take Etruscan Capua, the Etruscans' sphere of influence in the south shrank severely—all the way back to the north bank of the Tiber, across from Rome.

These setbacks had not seriously endangered or disrupted life in the rich cities of the Etruscan heartland. But the blows that started to fall soon after 400 B.C. struck at the very core of Etruscan civilization. The first great city to succumb to Rome, in 396 B.C., was Veii, long famous for its school of terra-cotta sculpture and for the engineering skills that had built its road network and its intricate system of cuniculi, the subterranean passages that prevented flood and drainage water from inundating local fields. But the Romans wanted neither sculptures nor cuniculi from the place that Livy called "the wealthiest city in Etruria." The conquerors coveted the town and its environs for long-term military and commercial reasons. Veii, only 12 miles north of Rome on a minor tributary of the Tiber, and linked by its web of roads to the other rich cities of southern Etruria, controlled riverborne trade and traffic on the lower Tiber as well as valuable salt pans at the Tiber's mouth.

For nearly half a century before Veii fell, its men had fought border skirmishes with neighboring

Games and Rites at a Pan-Etruscan Festival

Fiercely competitive and proudly independent, the cities of Etruria apparently had only one institution that expressed the Etruscans' communal identity as a people—a great annual festival attended by the rulers of the more important towns. The purpose of the gathering was to elect a titular chief, whose office was conferred for only one year and whose role was probably strictly symbolic.

The meeting place was the sacred grove of a sanctuary called, in Latin, the Fanum Voltumnae, at or near the city of Volsinii in central Etruria. The Etruscan name for the festival has been lost; the Latin name refers to Voltumna, the Etruscan god who was worshipped at this shrine. (Fanum means a place dedicated to a deity.)

The religious solemnities surrounding the election of a temporary chief for all Etruria lay at the core of the festival, but they were only a part of the proceedings. There were also athletic contests—acrobatic competitions, wrestling, boxing and chariot races as well as track and field events. These too were imbued with religious overtones, though the athletes themselves were not priests but mostly the slaves and servants of the nobles attending the festival. Merchants and traders also flocked to the Fanum Voltumnae to swap goods and commercial gossip at a fair that grew up around the games and sacred rites connected with choosing a leader.

Thus, over the course of centuries, the Fanum Voltumnae attracted citizens of all classes from the otherwise loosely related cities of Etruria, and no doubt gave them a certain sense of kinship and solidarity.

How the elected noble qualified for his supreme—though nominal—office, what his duties might have been, even what title the Etruscans gave him are uncertain. Roman records, however, convey a hint of his status; the Romans called him *sacerdos,* or priest,

This Sixth Century B.C. vase, 18 inches high, celebrates various sporting events that took place at the Fanum Voltumnae, the annual gathering of Etruscan cities. The boxers featured on this side fight to the music of a piper. Such a vase may have been one of the prizes given to winning athletes.

an indication that his function was primarily religious; there is no evidence that he had any political or military powers.

Just as obscure as the function of the *sacerdos* are the identities of the cities whose representatives convened at the Fanum Voltumnae. The Roman sources do not name the cities, but many scholars agree that they were the following: Caere, Tarquinii, Volsinii, Vulci, Clusium, Arretium, Perusia, Volaterrae, Veii, Rusellae, Vetulonia and Populonia.

Though the list of participants may have changed from time to time, the persistence of this great pan-Etruscan event is unquestioned; the festival of the Fanum Voltumnae occurred fairly regularly over a period of almost a thousand years. The Roman historian Livy wrote of several meetings held in the Fifth Century B.C., including one at which the king of Veii, outraged at not being elected *sacerdos,* flounced home, taking all his slaves with him; since the slaves were slated to be the principal contestants in that year's games, the entire spectacle must have suffered severely.

The last assemblies at the Fanum Voltumnae were held some 900 years later, in the Fourth Century A.D., long after the Etruscan cities had been destroyed or Romanized. According to Roman sources these later meetings still followed ancient custom, but had lost all real significance; they had become little more than an occasion for games and amusements.

Rome. The cause of these hostilities was the strategic town of Fidenae, which commanded a crossing of the Tiber north of Rome. The Romans had seized Fidenae more than once, but each time it revolted and went over to Veii. Finally, in 426 B.C., the Romans had reduced the town.

But even as Fidenae's forces went down to final defeat, they gave the Romans some bad moments. The most unnerving must have been a sortie by the defenders that Livy vividly described: "Suddenly through the open gates of Fidenae came pouring a stream of men armed with fire. It was like an army from another world—something never seen or imagined before. There were thousands of them, all lit by the glare of their blazing torches, and like madmen, or devils, they came rushing into the fray."

With the destruction of Fidenae, an all-out Roman attack on Veii seemed imminent. Long protected by its situation atop a tufa plateau guarded by steep cliffs, the city now erected its first walled fortifications. Huge blocks of masonry were set in place, and even though the siege that ended with the city's downfall is said to have lasted 10 years, the Romans could not bring the walls down. Only time has been able to breach them.

The tale of the city's defeat is told, again by Livy. When Veii's hour came, he wrote, "she fell by a stratagem and not by assault." The Romans dug a tunnel from their camp outside the city walls to a point beneath the sacred area of Veii. According to an old story—whose veracity, the historian admitted, was open to question—Roman soldiers huddled in the tunnel heard a priest tell the king of Veii, while in the act of sacrificing an animal, that he who carved up the animal's entrails would win the war. There-

upon the Roman soldiers broke into the sanctuary and snatched the entrails.

What followed, in Livy's account, was a scene that no doubt became familiar in other Etruscan cities destined to suffer the onslaught of Roman arms. The defenders of Veii, expecting an assault from outside the walls, were attacked from behind by the troops who had penetrated the city through the tunnel. "Buildings were set on fire as women and slaves on the roofs flung stones and tiles at the assailants. A fearful din arose: yells of triumph, shrieks of terror, wailing of women, and the pitiful crying of children; in an instant of time the defenders were flung from the walls and the town gates opened; Roman troops came pouring through." Then the victors spent the day "in the killing of Rome's enemies and the sacking of a wealthy city." But Livy does not fail to pay a Roman's tribute to the fallen foe. "Even her final destruction," he said of Veii, "was evidence of her greatness," and he added that during the long siege "she inflicted worse losses than she suffered."

No identifiable trace of the Roman tunnel has turned up in excavations at Veii. Perhaps the tale was invented after the Romans had found Veii's system of cuniculi. The Roman camp is believed to have been laid out on terrain above a number of these underground channels, which the people of Veii had foresightedly packed with rubble; possibly the Romans cleared one that burrowed under the city walls. Or perhaps the Roman tunnel never existed except as legend. The saga of Troy and all its heroes was familiar to both Etruscans and Romans, and the Romans may have looked upon the defeat of Veii as the fall of a latter-day Troy. The tunnel could have been their version of the Trojan-horse myth, and even

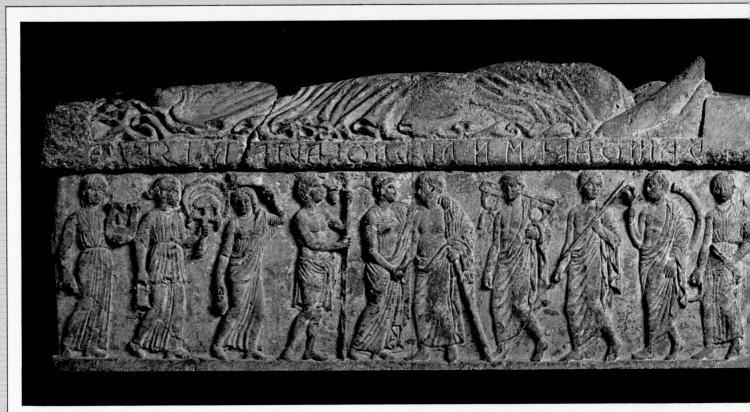

Mounting Gloom in a Shattered World

As Etruscan power began to wane before Roman assaults in the Fourth Century B.C., the exuberance that had once characterized Etruscan funerary art gave way to a pervading gloom. In better times the people of Etruria had envisioned the soul as passing to a garden of afterworld delights. Their happy anticipation of a tranquil eternity was evoked in numerous tomb paintings and in the warm attitudes of the couples sculpted in easy repose on coffin lids (page 59). But as doom approached, optimism gave way to the Greek outlook, with its view of death as an unhappy journey to a land of frightening shades. The details—shown in various perspectives—of the coffin on these pages capture the new mood of regretful leave-taking: the man and wife huddle under a covering, comforting each other.

On one side of this Third Century B.C. sarcophagus from Vulci, men and women solemnly gather for a farewell that is wistfully reminiscent of a wedding ceremony. At the center of the panel, the husband, holding a staff that symbolizes departure from life, clasps his wife's wrist while attendants pay homage to the couple: two girls hold musical instruments, others carry jewels and toilet articles, and youths carry emblems of the dead man's status as a high official—a curule chair, a scepter-like wand and a lituus (page 122). The female attendants—possibly slaves—wear Grecian clothing, and the young men wear Roman togas. The Etruscan inscription running the length of the seven-foot coffin—which contained only the woman's remains—identifies her as Ramtha Visnai.

Sustaining the warmth of their relationship in life, this middle-aged couple shares an immortal embrace on their bier. Draped over them is a toga, which a husband traditionally threw over the wedding bed—a poignant reminder of their earliest days together. The wife seems peacefully resigned, but her mate's face conveys both terrible grief and foreboding.

The scenes on the coffin's end-panels perplex modern scholars. Both seem to represent departure for the underworld. But in the top panel a bearded man is stepping aboard a chariot; if he is meant to be the husband, why is he seen clean-shaven on the sarcophagus lid at left? Below, two ladies on a mule-drawn cart are being observed by a winged spirit of death. One may be the wife, the other an attendant. The three faces above the vignettes echo temple antefixes, but the unsmiling visages lack the spontaneous joy of earlier counterparts.

This bronze helmet, taken as booty by the Greek commander after a naval victory in 474 B.C., carries a proud inscription: "Hiero, son of Deinomenes, and the Syracusans [dedicate] to Zeus the Etruscan spoils won at Cumae." The engagement at Cumae, a Greek colony near modern Naples, ended Etruscan maritime supremacy.

the story of the 10-year siege might be invention based on the Greeks' decade-long investment of Troy.

The taking of rich Veii sent a shudder throughout Etruria. But during the city's half century or more of struggles with Rome, Veii's neighbors had proffered little help. Capena and Falerii Veteres, powerful cities farther north in the Tiber valley, fought sporadically on Veii's side, possibly to defend their own access to the Veii-controlled salt pans at the mouth of the river, and for fear of Roman annexation. Caere, not far to the west of Veii, remained discreetly neutral; so did all the other Etruscan cities.

The fate of Veii may have nurtured the sense of gloom and apprehension that soon began to pervade all Etruscan tomb art. Violent death had swept down and obliterated the ordinary citizens of the town. Previously they had been able to look forward to a peaceful progression from this life to the next. But when the sword struck at the household, when blood was spilled in the streets and the temple, Etruscans recoiled. Priests and rulers were powerless to halt the march of events, and artists began to paint despair on the walls of the tombs.

The Romans, for all their ferocity, were a known quantity. The additional terror that descended on the Etruscans in about 390 B.C. was alien. So fearsome was this blow, struck from the north, that it temporarily drew even Romans and Etruscans together. Gallic hordes charged into northern Etruria and devastated Bologna, Marzabotto and other northern cities. According to Livy, Clusium, which also lay in the path of the invaders and had remained on good terms with the Romans, appealed to Rome for help —but the call went out too late. Clusium's citizens found "strange men in thousands at the gates, men the like of whom the townsfolk had never seen, outlandish warriors armed with strange weapons, who were already rumored to have scattered the Etruscan legions on both sides of the Po."

Clusium was besieged, but the main body of the Gauls bypassed the city and swept on toward Rome. A Roman army that tried to stop the invaders 10 miles outside the gates was routed. Caere, which had tried to get along with Rome even at the expense of Veii, its Etruscan sister-city, offered asylum to Rome's Vestal Virgins and holy objects before Rome, too, fell to the Gauls—who destroyed most of the city. Rome finally got rid of the invaders by the payment of tribute, and for safeguarding their Vestal Virgins the Romans acknowledged Caere as a friend and awarded its people honorary Roman citizenship.

When survivors of the attack on Rome looked around at the crumbled masonry walls and the charred buildings, a wave of public opinion urged evacuation of the ruined city and a move to Veii only 12 miles away. Veii had not been completely razed by its Roman conquerors, and the Romans were using its superb road network to move about their newly conquered territories. Only the eloquence of Camillus, a military leader appointed dictator during the Gallic crisis, persuaded citizens not to abandon Rome for the tempting cliff-bound site of Veii.

Recovering quickly, the Romans went about consolidating gains made before the Gauls had intervened. For several years they busied themselves establishing colonies in the lands wrested from Veii, and their army campaigned in the south. Taking advantage of these preoccupations, the Etruscans of Tarquinii, hoping to end—or at least curtail—Rome's dominance in central Italy, launched an attack in 358 B.C. A few years later, Falerii Veteres also took up arms against Rome, followed in 353 B.C. by Caere —whose leaders had chosen to forget their Roman friendship. Caere was quickly overcome but was not punished for its defection; instead, in view of its past services to Rome during the Gallic attack, it received a hundred years' truce. Two years later Tarquinii and Falerii Veteres were also defeated and also granted long truces—which the Romans hoped would help pacify these strategic regions and secure the cities as allies. In southern Etruria, resistance to the spreading might of Rome had almost ended.

But not quite. An army from the city of Volsinii had invaded Roman territory in 392 B.C. and was driven off. Nevertheless the city, appalled by the prospect of Roman domination, took up arms against Rome on three subsequent occasions during the next century or so. Each time it went down to defeat and was forced to come to terms with its conquerors. Volsinii's fifth and final collapse came in 265 B.C. when Roman leaders, answering the troublesome city's desperate call for help in quelling the revolt of freed slaves, decided to inflict a bloody penalty; Roman forces razed the city. The Romans then rebuilt it nearby, in a less easily defended position, and reestablished the local power of the nobility over the surviving inhabitants—but not before carting off 2,000 statues for the embellishment of Roman temples and public buildings.

The fate of Volsinii embodies two characteristic Roman policies for treatment of a humbled Etruscan city. The price of repeated rebelliousness against Rome was steep. On the other hand, the Romans were always very good at making friends or allies of their defeated enemies. The support given to the Volsinian aristocracy was not merely a gesture of generosity. As demonstrated by the treaties offered to Caere, Falerii Veteres and Tarquinii, the Romans were careful to cultivate the good will of local rulers once they

Bequests of Rituals to Rome

Among the Etruscan inventions passed on to Rome were many of its symbols of authority and its ceremonial observances. Some remained unaltered; others were modified to better serve the Romans' needs. For instance, in imperial times, the Romans laid out their town boundaries according to the sacred Etruscan rule: the perimeter had to be set by the furrow of a bronze plowshare that was drawn by oxen. The augurer's wand *(left)* that Etruscans held as they interpreted celestial omens became the Roman lituus. (In legend, Rome's founder, Romulus, carried a lituus while designing the city. By Christian times, the wand had become a crosier—a bishop's standard of office.) The fasces *(right)*, an ax with wooden rods bound around it, was used as a symbol of authority by Etruscan leaders; modified by Romans, it became the badge of power of kings and magistrates. In the 20th Century the fasces gave its name to Italy's Fascist Party, and became its emblem.

Paper thin, this 14-inch bronze priest's wand came from a Sixth Century B.C. tomb at Caere. An Etruscan soothsayer held one as he executed his duties.

123

A miniature model of an Etruscan
fasces, reconstructed from flakes of
rusted iron, came from Vetulonia.
Dating from 600 B.C. it is barely 10
inches high. In adopting this badge of
authority, the Romans replaced the
Etruscan double-bladed ax with a
single-bladed version of the weapon.

This three-foot-long section of a Roman frieze from the First
Century A.D. illustrates adherence to an Etruscan ritual—the
digging of a furrow that marked the boundaries of Aquileia, a
town founded by the Romans to the northeast of present-
day Venice. Four city fathers are witnessing the ceremony.

An Etruscan ruler seated on a foldable ivory stool faces the
statue of a goddess on this terra-cotta plaque from a tomb
in Caere. The scene, painted in 525 B.C., includes other
trappings of Etruscan royalty—the short purple toga and the
ivory scepter—that were adopted by Roman monarchs.

124

had been humbled, permitting them to remain in authority among their own people, and exacting their military and economic support whenever it was needed. But while allowing the Etruscans a degree of local autonomy, the Romans took the precaution of stationing troops at strategic points in Etruria. These military garrisons, together with the colonies that the Romans established in what had been Etruscan lands, served as reminders of the long, strong arm of Rome.

These were canny, intelligent tactics—an early example of the Romans' notable political skill. Eventually the talent helped them to master most of the ancient world.

The effectiveness of the system may very well have been proved in Etruria. Although several Etruscan cities revolted—Caere, for example, again broke its alliance in 273 B.C. and as a result had to cede half its territory—by 205 B.C. the Etruscans in general had accepted the new order. In that year a 30-year-old Roman consul, Publius Cornelius Scipio, who had already defeated Rome's Carthaginian archenemies

in Spain, was organizing a fleet for the expedition that was to humble Carthage once and for all. For this mighty task, whose fulfillment won the consul the title of Scipio Africanus, he needed a mountain of supplies, which he collected from all the peoples of the peninsula.

Livy listed the contributions of the Etruscan cities: Caere offered grain; Populonia, iron; Tarquinii, sailcloth; Volaterrae, grain and ships' fittings; Arretium, 3,000 shields, 3,000 helmets, and a total of 50,000 pikes, javelins and spears; Perusia, Clusium and Rusellae supplied fir for shipbuilding and a large quantity of grain.

From this laconic, business-like list comes the overwhelming image of a still-rich but subdued minority within an expanding world power that assumed its right to such resources as a fruit of conquest. That assumption marks the passing of a people—the end of the vivid life of free Etruscan cities, of some five and a half centuries of brilliant achievement and distinctive civilization.

Engineering to Master a Rugged Terrain

Much of the land once held by the Etruscans still bears the traces of their most remarkable and enduring legacy: their engineering accomplishments.

Undaunted by a diverse and often rugged terrain, the Etruscans connected their cities with a network of roads cut directly through rocky hills. They gouged out and carted away in baskets vast quantities of tufa and other debris to make thoroughfares level enough for their wheeled vehicles to negotiate easily. Where the road builders encountered waterways too deep to be forded, they spanned them with stout bridges that could bear the weight even of ox-drawn carts laden with goods for trade.

The engineers manipulated water as adroitly as they did the land. Roads were always designed to drain well, and towns had sewage systems. To expand the acreage that was suitable for farming, they diverted flooding streams into subterranean ducts.

Governed by a devotion to precision, the engineers relied on two surveying devices. One was an instrument called a *groma* with which they established straight lines and right angles in planning road intersections for towns on flat ground. The other was a leveling device called a *chorobates*, which may have guided them in laying even and solid foundations for buildings and in calculating infinitesimal but crucial grades for water-carrying conduits.

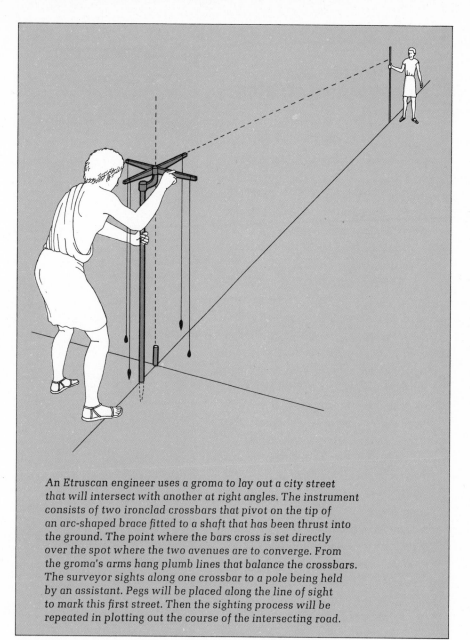

An Etruscan engineer uses a groma to lay out a city street that will intersect with another at right angles. The instrument consists of two ironclad crossbars that pivot on the tip of an arc-shaped brace fitted to a shaft that has been thrust into the ground. The point where the bars cross is set directly over the spot where the two avenues are to converge. From the groma's arms hang plumb lines that balance the crossbars. The surveyor sights along one crossbar to a pole being held by an assistant. Pegs will be placed along the line of sight to mark this first street. Then the sighting process will be repeated in plotting out the course of the intersecting road.

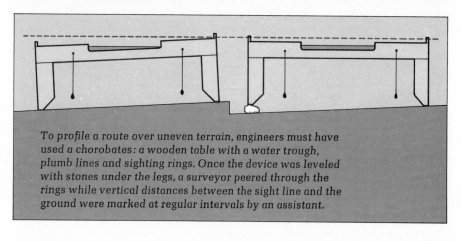

To profile a route over uneven terrain, engineers must have used a chorobates: a wooden table with a water trough, plumb lines and sighting rings. Once the device was leveled with stones under the legs, a surveyor peered through the rings while vertical distances between the sight line and the ground were marked at regular intervals by an assistant.

Dividing Hills and Spanning Rivers

The earliest of Etruria's roads inevitably took the form of narrow footpaths along and between the crests of tufa ridges; to circumvent natural obstacles they usually took circuitous routes along valleys and ravines, and crossed streams at natural fords.

But as the land became more densely settled, and as Etruscan commercial and military aspirations expanded, the cross-country pedestrian tracks were no longer adequate. Gradually they were replaced by properly engineered road and bridge systems. Supervised by Etruscan overseers, gangs of convicts or slaves hacked through hills of rock, creating thoroughfares wide enough to bear heavy vehicular traffic demanded by a growing economy.

Carved all the way down to bedrock wherever practicable, Etruscan roads were built with a channel running down one side to carry off rain water. Thus roadbeds were protected from being washed out by flash floods.

Such ingenious planning not only served the Etruscans well, it also laid the groundwork for Rome's glory. Many highways first built by Etruscans became the avenues by which Rome acquired and held its empire. Some of these same ancient routes still serve Italians today.

A road near Sovana, built by Etruscans around 600 B.C., cuts a deep path through a tufa hill. Over long years of service, hubs of wheeled vehicles have grooved the clifflike sides. On the left edge of the roadbed, now covered with weeds, runs a drainage ditch.

The northern abutment of a large bridge that once spanned a ravine near San Giovenale stands as testimony to the skill of Etruscan engineers. The facing stones have fallen off to reveal huge, dressed supporting blocks of tufa. The bridgehead, constructed before the Fourth Century B.C., is 23 feet wide and nearly 20 feet high.

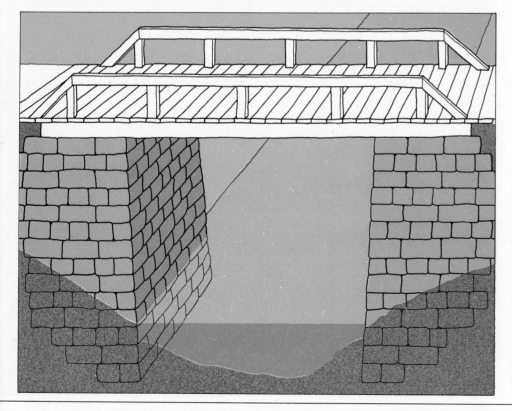

Because the deck of an Etruscan bridge was usually wood—requiring long timber supports that rested solidly on both abutments—its span depended on the length of available logs. Planks were set crosswise atop the timbers to form a sturdy roadway; guardrails lined the edges. The bridgeheads were set deep into the embankment. The exteriors of the approaches were faced with interlocking rectangular stones. Rows of headers, short ends of blocks facing outward, were set between stretchers, the blocks' long sides.

Draining Fields by Diverting Streams

Much of the topsoil of southern Etruria rested above an impermeable type of tufa that prevented absorption of water and made fields too soggy to farm. Etruscan engineers, therefore, devised underground drainage systems that led off accumulated water without eroding the precious loam. By carving long tunnels—known by the Latin name cuniculi—to collect and channel the water, the Etruscans made hundreds of acres of water-logged terrain arable, and diverted streams from courses that tended to flood fields or towns. Along the gently sloping route of a cuniculus that was under construction were vertical shafts that went from the surface down to the tunnel. The shafts served as entrances for the laborers and as exits for debris.

North of Veii, an 83-yard stretch of an Etruscan cuniculus, the Ponte Sodo, still diverts a part of the Valchetta River. The conduit was built in the Fifth Century B.C. to bypass a swampy horseshoe bend. The constant movement of water through the tunnel has considerably enlarged the passage.

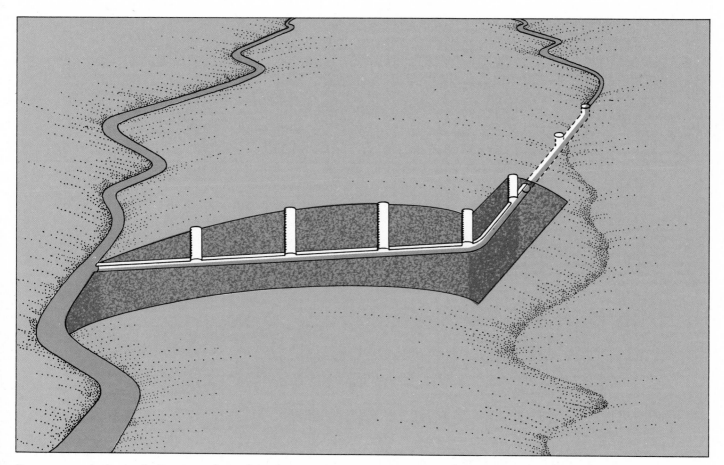

One way a cuniculus worked was to redirect the water of a stream (upper right) that tended to swell and overflow with torrential rainfalls into the valley below it. The stream was led into the cuniculus, which sloped gently—from right to left in this example—under the low hill. Then the water in the conduit was safely fed into a nearby river, at left. A duct of this sort—usually less than six feet high and about half a yard wide—had construction shafts every hundred or so feet; a laborer descended a shaft and hacked his way through the tufa toward another worker. For safety, the excavations were done during the dry season. The tufa substructure was strong enough so that underground supports were not needed.

Late in the 18th Century, Etruscology—the scholarly study of ancient Etruria's people based on the traces they left behind—was transmogrified into Etruscomania: a widespread and often mad fascination, both popular and academic, with all things Etruscan. During the 19th Century and into the 20th, the craze spread, and developed both a dark side and a bright one. On the dark side emerged a wave of fakery, thievery and destruction, accompanied by outrageous prices in the art market for genuine artifacts. On the bright side, new scientific procedures, cooperation among various disciplines and precise archeological methods have helped scholars solve some of the enigmas that have long cloaked these appealing people.

Since Roman times scholarly interest in the Etruscans has intensified or slackened in tandem with the general level of enlightenment in the world. But the enthusiasm reached a peak in 1955, sparked by a huge exhibition of Etruscan art and artifacts that was first assembled in Zurich and then toured Europe. The ferment generated by that show, visited by hundreds of thousands, has given no indication whatever of subsiding. The exhibition brought together for the first time treasures that previously had been scattered among the Vatican's Gregorian Etruscan Museum, the Villa Giulia in Rome, the musty Archeological Museum of Florence and Paris' Louvre.

With this great show, the "mysterious," "enigmatic" Etruscans were introduced in person, as it were, from Milan to Oslo: the fierce mustachioed warrior, the reclining noblewoman in her elegant attire, the devoted couple in embrace. Beside them were displayed other examples of Etruria's finest handiwork—the massive gold fibula from the Regolini-Galassi Tomb, a frieze of a horse race in furious action, an elegant bronze-wheeled incense burner, an avid satyr embracing a gently protesting maiden and a captivating pitcher shaped like a duck.

From the collection, for the first time, leaped the richness, the vitality, the humanity of a beguiling civilization that appealed mightily to European museumgoers. And once stimulated, the appetite for Etruscan artifacts became insatiable. Institutions and individual buyers clamored for them—and so thieves and forgers leaped in to help fill the gap between the supply of genuine grave goods and the demand of the marketplace. Knowing that many pieces for sale had been smuggled out of Italy, buyers hesitated to ask for such indispensable, verifying details as where a sculpture or a *bucchero* vase was found and the name of the finder. The result: stolen and skillfully forged items were sold alongside legitimate ones.

In the 1960s, for example, 34 paintings on terracotta plaques appeared in various dealers' galleries in Switzerland. One, though badly broken, showed the back of a chariot and part of a wheel. Another showed a tall bearded warrior standing before a shield, with a small ship in the background. A third featured an episode from the Trojan War. In general size and intensity of color, all the plaques—called *pinakes,* from the Greek word for picture—were similar to ones owned by the Louvre and the British Museum. The new *pinakes* were snapped up instant-

A woodland god and a maenad, his mortal partner, perform an orgiastic dance in this 11-inch terra-cotta sculpture by an Etruscan artist. Once a decoration on a Fifth Century B.C. temple, the statuette was one of hundreds of masterpieces assembled for a giant exhibit of Etruscan art that toured Europe in 1955 and 1956. The widespread modern fascination with the world of the Etruscans was set off by the show.

132

ly by private collectors and curators of museums.

Few questions were asked about the *pinakes'* origins and archeologists had no chance to study them. But after 1963, when photographs of some of the *pinakes* began to circulate, Etruscologists expressed doubts. First of all, the plaques showed no traces of preliminary undersketching. The Etruscans' characteristic painting technique required preplanning of designs—including the use of horizontal zone lines across the background to guide the artists in placing various figures. That was because the terra-cotta base being used was smeared with a plaster-like substance and painted while still wet so that the color impregnated the coating. Consequently, the paintings had to be completed quickly, and could not be revised effectively after they had dried.

Another peculiarity was the strange image of a gorgon on the shield in the so-called warrior-and-ship *pinaks*. Gorgons—female monsters from Greek mythology capable of turning men whose gaze met their eyes into stone—were popular in Etruscan art. But this gorgon was peculiarly painted, with white areas at the eyes, ears and cheeks. The only comparable example had turned up in 1955 on a wall painting that was exhibited in Zurich. Reasonably, some experts assumed that the new-found plaque was either a very valuable second find of a very rare type—or a fake inspired by the one-of-a-kind Zurich face. A forged piece that has but one authentic prototype generates much more skepticism than a fake artifact that has many similar models.

Other problems arose when the plaques were analyzed: on close examination, it turned out that one of the slabs had been broken before it was fired, an accident that in most circumstances would have im-

In the 1960s, Sweden's royal family was swept up in the rage for Etruscan discoveries. Working with two other ladies, Queen Louise (above, center) washed shards in San Giovenale; below, octogenarian King Gustaf VI Adolf assisted at a dig at Acquarossa.

pelled an Etruscan artisan to throw the thing away and make a new one. Occasionally, however, when an Etruscan artist did decide to mend a new piece that was cracking, he attached a small iron brace behind the flaw. But one of the Switzerland plaques had a remnant of a *bronze* brace—suggesting that at one time or other, some non-Etruscan hands had tinkered with the piece.

In the end, after scrutiny of both conspicuous clues and small ones, all 34 *pinakes* were pronounced fakes. One freewheeling collector found he had paid $1.2 million for his worthless imitations, and among those duped were several museums.

Nevertheless, oddities of style and material and technique are not of themselves sufficient to expose such fakes. Indeed, much of the charm of Etruscan art is its exuberant unexpectedness. The artisans indulged in stylistic quirks, and they often exaggerated certain features of a figure, or added touches of their own to the dress or the attitude of a statue inspired by Greek works.

Furthermore, each Etruscan city developed a style of its own, related perhaps but not identical to that of neighboring centers; and there was inevitably a broad diversity of abilities and skills among Etruria's artists during any given period. Artifacts of great refinement and high sophistication turn up in tombs and ruins next to very ordinary pieces produced by a simple neighborhood potter or metalsmith.

This great variety in Etruscan antiquities makes it relatively easy for the fine art of forgery to flourish. Even an expert hesitates to label an object as a fake if he is ignorant of its precise provenance (a connoisseur's term for place of origin); it might just be a whole new genre. An experienced archeologist will look at, say, a loop-handled jug decorated with animal heads as it emerges from a carefully conducted dig, shake his head in wry wonder and remark, "If I had seen that thing in a dealer's shop, I would have sworn it was a fake."

Fraud of the magnitude so frequently exposed by Etruscologists does have a bright side, in that it prompts prospective buyers to subject artifacts to careful scrutiny before laying out enormous sums. Fortuitously, the Research Laboratory for Archeology and the History of Art at Oxford University, dedicated to the detection of fraud and the authentication of the genuine, was founded in 1954—the year before the great Etruscan art show went on tour.

To test an Etruscan *pinaks,* for example, the laboratory first examines the pigments in the paint to compare them with genuine Etruscan substances, as well as the preparatory coat on which the paint has been applied. Finally, to determine the piece's age, a small sample of the terra cotta itself is subjected to a thermoluminescence test.

A TL test has less margin for error than the better-known carbon 14 test that also measures age. The TL test is based upon the fact that certain radioactive elements (radioisotopes) are naturally present in all fresh clay. But when the clay is fired, the radioisotopes' activity diminishes or disappears. Thus each newly fired pot or plaque begins life with a zero TL reading, or very near it. Gradually, however, over the piece's life span, its radioisotopes reactivate; the older a piece is, the greater its radioactivity. When a sample from a plaque is heated to 750° F., its radioactivity can be measured on a device that detects a radioactive glow. The luminescence gives a good index to the material's age.

It was this process that exposed the *pinakes* from Switzerland. Ultimately they all flunked the laboratory's tests; the pigments were new, as was the preparatory coat: the plaques had been made in the late 1950s by a skillful Italian forger whose work became all too familiar to dealers and museum curators.

No such brisk comeuppance befell the most notorious Etruscan forgeries in history: the great warriors in the possession of New York's Metropolitan Museum. There were three of these statues. One represented an old white-bearded warrior, nearly six feet eight inches tall. The second was a colossal helmeted head, four feet seven inches high. The third was the so-called Big Warrior, eight feet tall with a torso that was a bit short in proportion to his legs.

It was never the astonishing size of the Met's warriors that impaired their plausibility. The Roman writers Pliny and Plutarch had described the Etruscans' excellent techniques for fashioning—and then firing—figures of monumental size. Furthermore, the making of a certain very large quadriga, or four-horse chariot, inspired a legend all its own. Though the sculpture has never been found, the tale lives on.

As Plutarch recounted it, several Etruscan craftsmen in Veii were commissioned by an Etruscan king of Rome to sculpt the chariot. They shaped the clay and hauled it into a huge oven. There, instead of shrinking slightly, as clay usually does when its moisture evaporates, the statue began to rise like a loaf of bread. The chariot swelled so much that workmen had to dismantle the oven to get it out. Taking all this as an omen of the expanding power of their own city, the people of Veii threatened to revolt if the chariot were carted off to Rome.

So the fact that all three of the warrior statues were of giant proportions did not deter the Metropolitan from acquiring them between 1915 and 1921. They were shipped to New York in fragments that filled more than a dozen crates, were painstakingly reassembled and finally went on display in 1933, when the museum proudly opened a new Etruscan gallery. The great figures were an immediate hit with the public. But 28 years later embarrassed museum officials announced to the world that its three celebrated warriors were forgeries.

The unraveling of their history is one of the most romantic and bizarre tales in the annals of archeology. The first mention of the warriors came in a letter written to the Metropolitan in November 1915 by John Marshall, an English archeologist. Marshall, living in Rome as a buyer of Classical antiquities for the museum, could not contain his excitement about the possible purchase of the Old Warrior. "One thing I have arranged for, if a *permesso* for it can be obtained [from the Italian government]. It will make you groan to hear of it; the biggest T.C. [terra cotta] you or any reasonable being ever saw."

The Old Warrior was followed in 1916 by purchase of the Colossal Head and in 1921 by the Big Warrior. Marshall indicated in subsequent letters to the Metropolitan that he was having trouble ascertaining the origins of the giant statues and the circumstances of their discovery. He cautioned museum officials not to publish anything or to exhibit their new Etruscan treasures for the time being.

Marshall died in 1928, leaving numerous unanswered questions about the warriors, which finally went on show five years later. Soon there were rumblings from Italy. And in New York, dealer Piero

Text continued on page 138

The Case of the Forged Big Warrior

In producing their art, Etruscans paid little attention to the Classical ideals of proportion and shape that so preoccupied their Greek neighbors. Instead, they let inspiration and personal taste guide their hands. The resulting diversity of style and technique that characterizes their craftsmanship has made it relatively easy for forgers to create "Etruscan" artifacts. One of the most dramatic examples of fakery was the giant terra-cotta figure called the Big Warrior, acquired by New York's Metropolitan Museum of Art in 1921. Despite the sculpture's ungainly proportions and uncertain origins, considerations that raised the eyebrows of skeptical critics, it was not until 40 years after the purchase that a combination of scientific analysis and good old-fashioned sleuthing finally proclaimed it an enormous fraud—manufactured in 1918 by four Italian youths.

Just uncrated after its arrival at the museum, the Big Warrior's 20 pieces —weighing a total of 800 pounds—were put roughly in position. Because the artificers' kiln was small, the raw terra-cotta figure had been carefully broken up, then fired piece by piece—a method no Etruscan artisan would have required, since huge charcoal-burning ovens were used in ancient times.

A tiny five-inch bronze statuette in a Berlin museum was the genuine Etruscan prototype for the colossal fake. The counterfeiters themselves had never actually seen the object, only photographs of it in an art book.

136

Before its fall from grace, the eight-foot reconstructed warrior was a star of the Metropolitan Museum's Etruscan gallery, which opened in 1933. For 27 years, museumgoers and many experts overlooked the bogus statue's disproportionately long left arm and foreshortened torso—both the result of the forgers' inability to get a proper perspective on their work in progress within the confines of a small room.

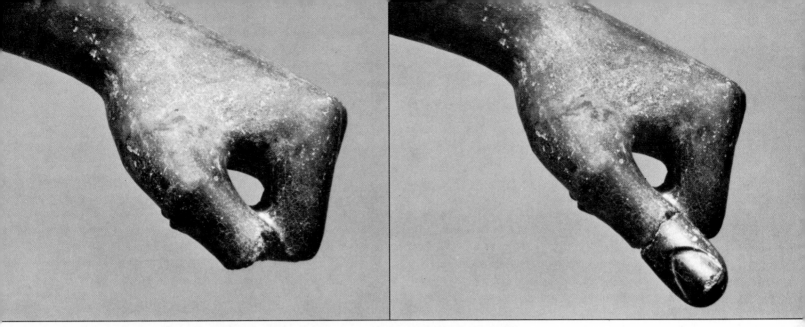

The tip of the thumb on the warrior's left hand had always been missing; one of the forgers had kept it as a souvenir when the statue was deliberately broken before being sold. After the surviving counterfeiter confessed, a museum representative made a plaster cast of the hand and took it to Rome. When the missing thumb fit the joint of the cast perfectly, the fraud was confirmed beyond all doubt.

In 1961 Alfredo Fioravanti, the only survivor of the quartet of forgers, was eking out a small but legal existence in Rome repairing minor works of art. Unashamed of his early misdeed, he had readily confessed his part in the hoax to those who tracked him down, but added that his involvement had not paid very well. The museum, he said, had put up $40,000 for his masterpiece, but all he had received from the shady middlemen was "a few hundred."

Tozzi wrote a vague warning letter to Gisela M. A. Richter, curator of Classical art at the museum. Tozzi said that he had information of interest to museum officials; they should try to meet soon. The note ended with a nonsentence consisting of three names: Fioravanti-Riccardi Bros.-Teodoro.

Riccardi had been familiar to the museum. Marshall's former secretary, in a report to Met officials, had alerted them to the fact that two self-proclaimed excavators, "the Riccardi brothers, are watched by the government because they are known to know Etruria thoroughly and to have made excavations with and often without a permit." As for Fioravanti, when the Met asked about him, the secretary reported that he had been a taxi driver in Rome for years and that he did not "sound much like an artist."

In December 1937 a Rome journal published an article by Massimo Pallottino, who was to become dean of Italian Etruscologists, brusquely denouncing all three sculptures as fakes, and even identifying some genuine examples from which they might have been copied. But somehow the article was never picked up in the United States.

As the years passed and thousands filed solemnly through the Met's Etruscan gallery, a scholarly controversy smoldered. In the 1940s Harold W. Parsons, an American art expert and buyer operating in Rome, expressed his own reservations. Similar doubts were voiced throughout scholarly circles in Rome, where the scent of fakery was growing strong; and in 1954 Pallottino repeated his charges.

In 1958 Parsons wrote to inform the Met that he had become acquainted with a man named Fioravanti, who proudly claimed to have forged an Etruscan terra cotta called the Copenhagen *Kore*—a draped

Among the proudest possessions of New York's Metropolitan Museum of Art, this 18-inch Greek vase was probably stolen from an Etruscan tomb and smuggled out of Italy. The museum acquired it in 1972, after it had passed through many hands, for one million dollars—more than any similar piece had ever fetched. The urn, dating from 500 B.C., bears the signatures of the painter, Euphronios, and potter, Euxitheus.

female figure—which had found its way to display at the Ny Carlsberg Glyptothek, a museum in the Danish capital. In this letter Parsons did not connect Fioravanti with the Met's warriors. But the following year, an Italian archeologist visiting New York refused even to look at the warriors, saying to the museum's red-faced curator of Greek and Roman art, "How can I, when I know the man who made them?"

At about the same time another museum official, Joseph V. Noble, read that a group of German scientists had managed to duplicate the Greek—and the Etruscan—method for imparting black to their fired pottery. The most significant aspect of the technique, Noble noted, was that it did not employ manganese. Manganese had been utilized by the ancient Egyptians, never by the Etruscans. Guessing that a forgery might contain manganese, Noble decided to have the black surfaces on the Met's warriors tested.

Furthermore, he undertook to examine personally some of the world's other giant terra cottas. In 1960 he and Metropolitan curator Dietrich von Bothmer went to Europe. Both were immediately struck by the observation that all the genuine large Etruscan sculptures incorporated ventholes that had permitted circulation of air during the drying and firing process. For example, the famous striding Apollo of Veii, believed to have been sculpted by the Etruscan master Vulca, was constructed, Noble noted, "like a chimney, with big holes for the intake of air between his legs and a large opening in his back, between his shoulder blades." This was damning evidence indeed, since the Met's Old Warrior had no ventholes, and the other two pieces had only very small holes that would have been insufficient to keep them from exploding had they been fired in one piece.

Finally, in January 1961 another letter to the Metropolitan arrived from Parsons. Enclosed was a deposition of a confession that Alfredo Adolfo Fioravanti, hounded and cajoled by Parsons, had made before the United States consul in Rome. In the statement, Fioravanti admitted to being one of the creators of the three Etruscan pieces. He still had in his possession, he said, the missing left thumb of the Big Warrior, which he had snapped off as a memento after the sculpture was fired.

In what must have been one of the strangest encounters in archeological history, the Metropolitan's von Bothmer and the 78-year-old Fioravanti met in Rome in February 1961. As von Bothmer proffered a plaster cast of the Big Warrior's left hand, which he had brought with him from New York, Fioravanti produced a clay thumb and extended it. The thumb fitted the hand perfectly.

Then the whole story poured out. Fioravanti had been trained as a tailor. His avocation was bicycle racing, and through that he met a young man named Riccardo Riccardi and his cousins Teodoro and Virgilio Angelino. All three worked in a family ceramics business, restoring ancient pots for antique dealers. Fioravanti was persuaded to join them, and his tailor's fingers adapted quickly to the potters' trade. Fioravanti insisted that he and his young friends had fallen into forgery by accident.

By the time von Bothmer and Fioravanti met, spectrographic tests of the glaze on the Met's warriors had proved that the black on all three had indeed been achieved with manganese. Though Fioravanti knew nothing of these tests, when he was questioned about the glaze he remembered that it had been done with *biossido di manganese*.

He and the cousins had first modeled the full figures from the ground up, just as the Etruscans had done. But the forgers had been forced to break the terra-cotta statues into small pieces before firing; because they lacked the giant kilns of the Etruscans, they had to rely on the little four-by-three-by-three-foot models used for producing modern ceramics.

At last, Fioravanti offered an appealingly human explanation for two details that had long troubled some experts: the missing right arm of the Old Warrior and the truncated shape of the Big Warrior. The first aberration occurred, he said, because the sculptors could not agree on an appropriate position for the right arm; they simply decided not to make one. The second came about because of the low ceiling in the workshop they had rented in Orvieto. By the time they reached the Big Warrior's waist, it was clear there wasn't going to be enough room for his head, so they shortened the torso.

Despite scholarly detective work and new technology, Etruscan fakes and forgeries remain on exhibition in most of the world's museums. But many curators and collectors now. insist upon submitting ancient artifacts to scientific analysis before they buy. The forgers, however, have become increasingly wily, too. One of the scholars at the Villa Giulia has suggested that somewhere in Europe, probably in Italy, a brilliant forger is operating with an illegal nuclear energy source; he uses it to irradiate fired clay, so that even a thermoluminescence test could be thrown off. "This man can paint like an Etruscan or like a Greek," the scholar said. "If his vases, which look perfect, were properly irradiated, they would fool 90 per cent of the world's high market."

Finally, to further confound the marketplace, illegal genuine finds and expert forgeries are often mixed together in job lots right at the site of a dig.

Theft of material from tombs and sacred areas began, no doubt, as far back as Etruscan times, as local robbers went in search of treasure. Certainly the practice was widespread when Romans conquered Etruscan cities during the Fourth and the Third centuries B.C., pillaging as they went. Until the late 19th Century A.D. the losses, though deplorable, were comprehensible. As early as the First Century A.D., the Romans enacted a law against looting ancient sites, but the Roman statute was never enforced and the treasure hunting went on. The unfortunate result was that most of the Etruscans' gold, ivory and silver artifacts have vanished.

Today's thieves invade old burial sites and steal pots, hack heads from sarcophagus figures and grind up *bucchero* fragments to use as the ingredients for new fake pots. But they also add to the confusion by stealing catalogued artifacts and black-marketing them to unscrupulous or unwitting customers. In 1962 the town of Tuscania had to cancel opening ceremonies for a museum of Etruscan relics because thieves stole the entire collection the night before the show's debut. In 1963 culprits armed with hammers, chisels, electric saws and steel wire cut away frescoes from four newly opened tombs in Tarquinia. In 1971 the museum of Chiusi lost 100 pieces in one night.

Among the most proficient thieves are the *tombaroli*—the peasant tomb robbers. Mostly farmers and shepherds, they know the territory intimately and while away dull winter months by robbing the tombs they have come upon in the course of planting, plow-

Eyes That See into Unopened Tombs

Archeologists estimate that through the centuries 85 per cent of Etruria's tombs were plundered by thieves. As a result, the slow and costly conventional methods of excavating newly located burial sites are often fruitless. In 1955 an Italian named Carlo M. Lerici took the gamble out of tomb explorations. He invented a probe that penetrates into a tomb from aboveground and shoots photographs of the interior—like those below of the Tomb of the Warrior at Tarquinii.

Lerici's system starts with an electronic mechanism that detects underground hollows. Once the presence of a tomb is established, a periscope is sunk through a drilled hole to see if photographing or opening the tomb would be worthwhile. During the first two decades of the system's use, almost 7,000 tombs were examined in this way, and 560—most of them with valuable artifacts—were opened.

After locating a burial site, one of Lerici's assistants inserts a photographic probe (left) into a stabilizing collar placed over a drilled hole. Pictures of the tomb's interior will be taken at intervals of 30° by the probe's camera, lighted by a stroboscopic flash. At right, a colleague scans the inside of a tomb with a periscope that rotates like a submarine's.

Adjacent shots taken inside the Tomb of the Warrior produced the first photographic evidence of Etruscan murals on three walls.

ing and herding. Archeologists have been known to follow *tombaroli*—at a discreet distance; since there are more robbers than archeologists, it stands to reason that some experienced *tombaroli* will lead them to diggable sites. Their detection technique is simple and efficient. When a *tombarolo* comes upon a promising mound or hillock, he stamps on the top. If he feels a tremor or senses an echo, he knows there is empty space below. Then he probes with a pointed steel rod until it hits stone—the top of a tomb—or breaks through into a hollow area.

Having recruited a couple of companions, he and his cohorts make it the work of a single night to dig out the entrance and sack a tomb. The vast physical expanses of Etruscan necropolises and the inability of the Italian government to patrol known sites effectively facilitate the work of the *tombaroli*. Nonetheless, they are often caught and prosecuted for their activities, though rarely fined or sent to jail. A well-meaning organization of citizens calling themselves Gruppi Archeologici d'Italia did sterling vigilante work in the early 1970s, guarding known sites from the ravages of the *tombaroli,* but this volunteer corps —apparently overwhelmed by the magnitude of its job—grew discouraged and less active.

Tomb robbing goes on at a steady pace. From the hands of *tombaroli* the material moves to middlemen, who smuggle it into Switzerland. There it is restored and provided with spurious documents of legitimate exit. Then it moves into the overheated financial circles of museums and private collectors.

Once a genuine artifact has been launched on the price escalator it can lose its value to the serious student. He may look at it in a museum, if the fragment was fortunate enough to come to rest in such an accessible place, but it will tell him little unless it was properly excavated and assessed in the course of correct archeological procedure. To "read" it, the student must know how it lay in relation to other finds, its precise provenance, its approximate date. But out of context, it tells him little.

"Removing a pot from a tomb is like cutting a button from a suit," an Italian archeologist has said. "The button by itself won't do you much good, and you can no longer wear the suit."

When tomb robbing was just a treasure hunt, it was not much more of a crime than jumping a land claim. But from the moment scholars began using artifacts as priceless tools for writing history, such theft became comparable to the willful destruction of an invaluable ancient archive.

In contrast to the skulduggery of earlier days, modern digs are meticulous and slow. At a site like Graviscae, for example, a crew of bare-torsoed Italian pickmen directed by an Etruscologist probe delicately at the soil, their trained hands alert to the feel of an ancient structure. Beside them in the sweltering summer heat, young archeologists in sandals, blue jeans and bikini tops watch each cautious blow.

With tape measures and grid paper they record the position, size and superimposition of each tumbled rock and broken shard. Pottery fragments go into plastic bags marked with the exact location and level of the find, the time of day, the date. Larger bits go into specially built wooden boxes, similarly marked. All are carted off to workrooms in nearby archeological museums, where the contents of boxes and bags are painstakingly catalogued, restored and translated into solid information.

Called The Cowboy for its sombrero-like hat, this terra-cotta sculpture was a tantalizing jigsaw puzzle for restorers. The first fragments came to light near Siena in 1966. More bits turned up over the next five years, and in 1972, 15 or so pieces were glued together with a gray mastic that fills the seams; the missing lap section shows up here as the white area. Gathering the pieces had been especially taxing because the statue had been smashed and scattered by Etruscans fleeing invaders around 500 B.C. If standing, the figure would measure just over five feet—average height for an Etruscan male.

Such methods can produce near-miracles. Beginning in 1966 at a site called Poggio Civitate south of Siena, nine summer expeditions supervised by an American from Bryn Mawr College exposed an enormous Etruscan sanctuary more than 4,300 square yards in size and dating from the Sixth Century B.C. The sanctuary had been destroyed by the Etruscans themselves shortly before 500 B.C., and the decorated roof tiles, antefixes and triumphant figures that adorned the temple ridgepoles had been scattered across the area, buried in trenches adjoining the formerly sacred confines, or used as fill for an agger, or earthen wall. The barrier had been erected to indicate that the former holy place had been deconsecrated, for reasons unknown, and sealed off forever.

The reconstruction of one ridgepole figure, known affectionately as The Cowboy, is illustrative of modern archeological methods. During the first two years of the dig, students noticed that several fragments of terra cotta that they had found scattered over the sanctuary seemed to belong together. In 1968 a strangely shaped piece that looked like the wide, upturned brim of a ten-gallon hat appeared amid debris at the west side of the court. The hat's tall crown had been dug up the year before, but without the brim it had not seemed to relate to the other pieces. Many more segments—enough to give form to the figure —were unearthed during the three following seasons.

Fifty years before, even 20 years before, such a mixture of random bits no doubt would simply have been discarded as incomprehensible, or else piled into unmarked crates to wait indefinitely in a museum storeroom for someone with the time and energy to try to make sense of them. In today's brighter climate, a well-known Florentine Etruscologist,

Guglielmo Maetzke, was able to find funds to have expert Italian restorers piece The Cowboy back together and then to install him in a small new museum on the central square of Siena.

Archeologists have profited enormously in recent decades not only from more meticulous scholarship and heightened awareness of the importance of the past, but also from a growing cooperation among geologists, anthropologists, historians and etymologists, thereby bringing the Etruscan cities, their history and their life closer to real understanding. In addition, new or newly refined techniques have been borrowed from other fields. From military reconnaissance came the aerial photograph; from geophysical prospecting for oil or water came the stratigraphic drill that can bore straight down and bring up a core of stratified earth, rock and pottery fragments.

A spin-off from the space industry was a highly sensitive instrument called a magnetometer, which measures the magnetic intensity of the ground—a help in locating buried artifacts. Man-made masonry has a different magnetic pull from ordinary earth, as does material once exposed to intense heat, such as household ovens and pottery kilns. The instrument responds to the variation in magnetism below ground, and can indicate where diggers ought to dig.

Another new dimension in archeology goes back to the years before World War I. Italian army engineers had helped cartographers and archeologists to identify natural and ancient man-made features in Rome and on the coast with the aid of photographs taken from balloons. The primitive approach had been much refined by the time of World War II: British and American flyovers produced aerial photos that were turned over to archeologists after the war for a whole new look at Italy's buried treasures.

One clue to reading an archeological aerial is that vegetation on top of buried masonry grows more sparsely, and appears in photographs somewhat lighter, than adjacent herbiage. The entrance to a tomb usually has a deeper layer of dirt that sustains more lush growth. Vegetation atop ancient canals, ports, moats and silt-filled waterways of any kind is thick and dark. Thus, educated reading of an aerial photo can trace an ancient road, or locate a lost city, a buried monument or a hidden tomb.

Often, inspired amateurs rather than professional archeologists develop and apply new techniques. One such was Julian Whittlesey, a retired architect who, late in the summer of 1974, made low-level aerial photos for a joint American-Italian diving team engaged in a study of ancient ports (pages 147-153). Whittlesey devised an elaborate system for hitching an electronically controlled camera to a low-flying balloon and floating it over areas that interested the diver-archeologists. Team members, standing nearby and watching the position of the balloon, relayed a signal to Whittlesey's wife when they wanted her to push the remote-control shutter button to take pictures. The balloon pictures were better than photographs taken from low-flying planes or helicopters. For one thing, prop wash disturbs the water or vegetation below; for another, aerials taken at altitudes as low as 30 feet above the water bring into view landmarks that are indistinguishable on higher aerial shots. Whittlesey's photographs enabled the diving team to locate underwater masonry, view the topography of the adjacent coast and trace extensions between the submerged masonry and remnants that had turned up on dry land.

It was another impassioned amateur, a Milanese named Carlo M. Lerici, who in the mid-1950s introduced in Italy the techniques of geophysical exploration to locate and probe Etruscan tombs. A retired engineer, Lerici decided to pursue his lifelong passion for archeology. His basic tools were a few dry-cell batteries, a lot of wire, some metal stakes and a galvanometer to measure the amount of resistance to the passage of an electrical charge.

Lerici started with aerial photographs, but a mound clearly visible in a picture taken from above can be extremely difficult to locate amid the underbrush, especially since much of the land being studied is under cultivation and subject to seasonal plowing. Hence his electrical equipment. When Lerici arrived in a promising area, he drove the metal stakes into the ground about 18 feet apart. To each stake he connected wires running back to the batteries and the galvanometer, and sent a small electrical charge into the stakes. The principle he was exploiting is simple: water and damp earth are good conductors of electricity; air is not. When the charge transmitted from the batteries encountered any resistance—an underground hollow—the needle on the galvanometer registered high. Fluctuations of the meter were plotted on a plan of the area, and they unfailingly revealed the center of each underground cavity.

To this technique, Lerici added an ingenious device of his own: a cylinder fitted with a tiny camera that had a remote-controlled shutter trigger and a built-in light source. After removing a narrow core of earth from the precise center of an Etruscan tomb, doing negligible damage, he would insert the camera-equipped tube through the hole, and take a series of photographs that indicated not only the general condition of the buried tomb's interior but also its contents. One quick look at the negatives, or through a periscope that Lerici later developed, would indicate whether at some time the tomb had been looted or defaced, and whether or not it contained enough material to warrant excavation.

In the first three years of operation Lerici and a field crew discovered and photographically explored 2,500 Etruscan tombs, mostly near Caere and Tarquinii, and turned up 6,000 pieces of Etruscan and Greek art. Always, of course, they dreamed of finding an Etruscan tomb with frescoes as spectacular as the Tomb of the Lionesses at Tarquinii, opened in 1874. Then in one glorious year—1958—Lerici and his men found seven rich sites. The most famous was revealed just as Rome was preparing to host the 1960 Olympic Games. Its frescoes of athletes caused it to be named the Tomb of the Olympiads. By 1974 Lerici's crew had explored many of the 10,000 tombs thought to be in the necropolis near Tarquinii, and identified some 60 that contained valuable frescoes.

Such material discoveries, justifiably greeted with cries of joy, can actually add less to Etruscology than poorer finds, such as those at Poggio Civitate, at Graviscae and at Acquarossa. At Poggio Civitate, for example, where The Cowboy's many fragments were found, learning that the sanctuary was deliberately destroyed added an incomparably important piece of the puzzle about Etruscan civilization; it was a clue to the narrative of history. The sanctuary's ruination can be dated reliably—on the basis of accompanying pottery types and styles—to very near 500 B.C., a period that coincides with the destruction and abandonment of another Etruscan site 60 miles to the south: a place now called Acquarossa. Though Poggio Civitate was in north Etruria and Acquarossa in the south, both came to a sudden end during the unstable period of Etruscan federation. Scholars will be pondering the meaning of that fact for years to come.

How many more such details of Etruscan history still lie buried, after all the centuries, no one knows of course; but hidden clues continue to come to light. Toward the end of 1974 the Italian police, hot on the trail of *tombaroli,* rushed into a valley called Greppe di Sant'Angelo on the very edge of Caere. There, having deterred the *tombaroli,* they ordered half a hill bulldozed down. Then they called in archeologists to announce that they had found what the robbers had been seeking: a previously unexplored cluster of Etruscan tombs. Among them were rectangular cells cut into cliffs, with elaborately carved false doors and artful architectural sculptures that resembled those of the cliff-cut graves of Norchia, Castel d'Asso and Sovana, to the north.

All the tombs had long ago been efficiently looted, but archeologists did find, in an area just outside and slightly below the tomb level, a kind of funeral dump that had not been vandalized. Its treasures included two curly haired stylized stone lions and—though so badly damaged they are difficult to see—a series of reliefs sculpted with lions and griffins pursuing and bringing down deer and other game.

Most stunning of all was a stone sculpture of an Etruscan demon-god, perhaps a portrait of Tuchulcha. The Greppe di Sant'Angelo figure seemed far less fearsome, less sinister, than the other known Etruscan images of spirits of death, and some students wondered aloud if the figure might be a hitherto unknown demon-god of the Etruscans. The sculpture

could be one of a kind—a spectacular discovery. Or it could be a fake seeded into the terrain years ago. But why, if it is truly Etruscan, is this demon-god so relatively pleasant and benign, so unlike the horrid versions of the other paintings and bas-reliefs?

"Possibly, the sculptor of this figure was a young man, an optimist," said Professor Mario Moretti of Rome's Villa Giulia, as he stood near the excavation in 1974. "He knew about death and demons, but for a young man these are all far away. So he made a less fearsome figure, because he was not yet afraid." Moretti agreed that this stone demon might not even be Tuchulcha. But the world wants labels, and that one seemed most logical at first glance. "We must study," said Moretti, "because we do not yet know for sure."

As the professor spoke, standing on a mound of dirt near the excavation, there was the soft sound of snuffling in the underbrush. The site of the new discovery had recently been turned into a breeding farm for wild boar—the hunting of which the Etruscans loved so much, the game they rendered so often in paintings and on the sides of their sarcophagi.

Here, on this same spot, Etruscan families had come to pay respect to the dead and perhaps to watch the sunset. Here they hunted boar, feasted, drank and reveled in the joy of life, the view, the security of their tufa hills. From here they walked, by some path now lost, to the homes that crowned the cliffs and surveyed the glittering sea. Their presence is still alive in the landscape. Standing on this spot a visitor easily imagines a bearded man and an elegantly draped lady wending their way across the crumbs of broken tufa. And the visitor yearns to say, in the language that was theirs, "Good evening. I salute you."

Aerial Views for Probes under the Sea

The maritime history of the Etruscans has yet to be written. That they were a great sea power is amply documented in Classical writings, but until very recently physical traces of their naval and industrial centers near harbor areas had been impossible to find. Much of what the Etruscans left behind was obscured by the later building of people who followed them; and the sea itself—its level slowly rising and eating away at the shore—obliterated the rest.

Finally, though, solid material for that history is coming to light. In 1970 a group of American archeologists combined techniques of aerial photography and marine exploration to probe the shores of Populonia. Their most intriguing underwater find—a piece of wood carbon-dated to the Ninth Century B.C.—encouraged them to pursue the search. Four years later a team of Italian scientists joined the Americans to chart more of western Italy's ancient coast, including Pyrgi. Slowly they began to find what probably once were Etruria's harbors.

Julian Whittlesey, inventor of a balloon mounting for a camera, helps a colleague walk the rig into the harbor at Pyrgi. Pictures can thus be taken at altitudes from 30 feet to 2,000 feet. When the camera is aloft, a balancing device keeps the lens aimed downward and a remote control snaps the shutter. Exposures must be made early in the morning when the wind is low and sunlight does not glare off the water.

At Populonia, a diver uses the nozzle of a hydraulic dredge to clear the area where an ancient coffin was found. The dredge sucks in the sand and mud surrounding objects and deposits the sediment well behind the diver.

At 100 feet over Pyrgi subtle color differences are visible in the water. The darker areas are shallow and rocky; the clear band (center) marks a channel used by ancient ships. The rectangle (lower left) is the fish tank or tower.

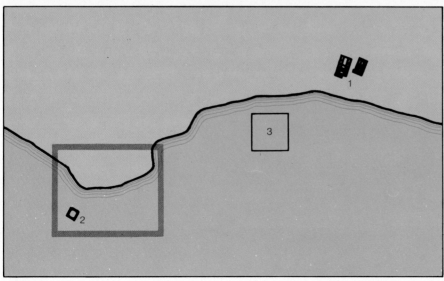

A simplified map of Pyrgi's modern coast indicates the sites of three ancient ruins—one inland and two offshore: the place where the gold tablets with Etruscan and Phoenician texts were discovered (1), the fish tank or tower base (2) and the submerged remains of a Roman city (3). The portion of the map outlined in the large rectangle corresponds to the area covered by the photograph above.

Team members, led by Anna McCann and Nino Lamboglia (center), compare photographs with a map before deciding where divers should be sent.

Exploring Pyrgi's Submerged Ruins

Aerial photographs taken over Pyrgi helped confirm a theory held by the archeologists: that the waterfront of Etruscan and Roman times had crumbled and the sea had engulfed both land and man-made objects on it, including a dock and a squarish structure that may have been either the base of a tower or a tank where live fish were stored.

After more than a week of effort, these were the only things the searchers could find; then they got lucky. On the last weekend at Pyrgi, a nearby tile factory shut down. The heavy effluents veiling the sea bottom cleared, and divers were able to see—and the team to photograph—the massive architectural remains of a city of Imperial Rome: marble columns, brick walls and arches, and the vestiges of a wide road.

Two divers—the swim fin of one showing at the center, the body of the other vaguely discernible underwater at lower left—explore the sea bottom off the coast of modern Santa Severa, the site of ancient Pyrgi. The floating inner tube supports a motorized pump connected by the yellow hose to the hydraulic dredge used by one of the divers. The water foams white where waves strike submerged Roman walls.

A Major Payoff at Populonia

Combing the sea bottom off modern Populonia, the site of Etruscan Fufluna, yielded striking results. According to Classical literature, Fufluna was the heart of Etruria's iron-processing industry. But the harbor's original contours were a mystery. So the Tuscan port scientists applied the most advanced techniques to its underwater explorations at Populonia.

In the course of two studies, four years apart, they established that the coastline had receded as much as 260 feet, and were able to add substantial details about Fufluna's general layout. The crowning triumph was the discovery of a shattered pot (page 153) that was distinctively Etruscan.

Located today almost on the edge of the sea at Populonia, this Etruscan tumulus was part of a Seventh Century B.C. cemetery now partly underwater. The necropolis once extended almost 98 feet beyond the modern waterfront.

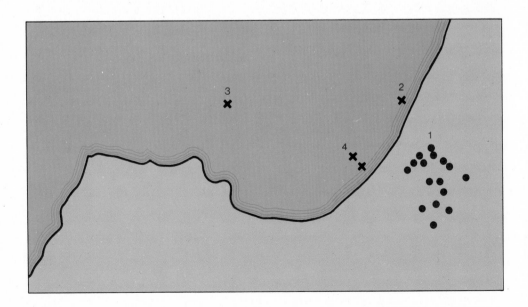

All but one of the four sites marked on this map—covering an area of one square mile just north of Populonia—stood on dry land in ancient times.

In 1970 the explorers were drawn to this area by the visible remnants of the Etruscan necropolis (1) and the extensive slag heaps near the shore. Divers soon discovered a submerged sarcophagus (2) and—most rare—wood (3), from what may have been a barge, carbon-dated at 800 B.C. Four years later the team returned and probed the sea bed (4) to find how far the slag layer could be found beyond the present shoreline (diagram opposite).

A diver uses a water-jet probe to pierce the sand and silt over solid objects, and measure how deep they lie buried.

Buoyed by inflated duffel bags, an open-ended steel caisson is guided to a site. There the bags are collapsed and the drum sinks to the bottom. One diver will then climb inside to dredge sand and silt from found objects. After the bags are refilled with compressed air, the drum is moved to the next site.

A diagrammatic sketch—not drawn to scale—shows the two spots plumbed by the caisson technique in the photograph above and indicated as number 4 in the map opposite. The drum farthest out (A) hit nothing, but the other (B) struck a long deposit of slag (C) that lay almost four feet below the sea floor. Water-jet probes established that the slag, deposited by Etruscan smelters at the waterfront, extended 260 feet from today's shore.

Ghostly divers hover close to the sarcophagus of an Etruscan child. The coffin, now overgrown with Poseidon grass, was entombed in a part of Populonia's cemetery that today lies underwater. Twenty sandstone blocks found near the sarcophagus may have been part of the burial vault.

Using a crayon, a diver charts on a plastic sheet the exact location of new-found logs. Measuring rods laid in a grid help him draw to scale. These logs may have been part of an Etruscan barge used to carry iron ore from nearby Elba to the Fufluna smelting works. The find was left in place for further study; the wood is 2,800 years old and if raised to the surface and allowed to dry out would disintegrate.

A broken wine pitcher was discovered lying close to the pieces of wood shown on the opposite page. Easily identified as bucchero pottery, a type that was the exclusive product of Etruscan artisans, the pot fragment has led archeologists to surmise that the wooden barge remnants uncovered near it must also have been Etruscan.

The Emergence of Man

This chart records the progression of life on earth from its first appearance in the warm waters of the new-formed planet through the evolution of man himself; it traces his physical, social, technological and intellectual development to the Christian era. To place these advances in commonly used chronological sequences, the column at the

Geology	Archeology	Billions of Years Ago	
Precambrian earliest era		4.5	Creation of the Earth
		4	Formation of the primordial sea
		3	First life, single-celled algae and bacteria, appears in water
		2	
		1	

		Millions of Years Ago	
			First oxygen-breathing animals appear
		800	
			Primitive organisms develop interdependent specialized cells
		600	Shell-bearing multicelled invertebrate animals appear
Paleozoic ancient life			Evolution of armored fish, first animals to possess backbones
		400	Small amphibians venture onto land
			Reptiles and insects arise
			Thecodont, ancestor of dinosaurs, arises
Mesozoic middle life		200	Age of dinosaurs begins
			Birds appear
			Mammals live in shadow of dinosaurs
			Age of dinosaurs ends
		80	
			Prosimians, earliest primates, develop in trees
Cenozoic recent life		60	
		40	Monkeys and apes evolve
		20	
		10	Ramapithecus, oldest known primate with apparently manlike traits, evolves in India and Africa
		8	
		6	Australopithecus, closest primate ancestor to man, appears in Africa
		4	

Geology	Archeology	Millions of Years Ago	
Lower Pleistocene oldest period of most recent epoch	**Lower Paleolithic** oldest period of Old Stone Age	2	Oldest known tool fashioned by man in Africa
		1	First true man, Homo erectus, emerges in East Indies and Africa
			Homo erectus populates temperate zones

		Thousands of Years Ago	
Middle Pleistocene middle period of most recent epoch		800	Man learns to control and use fire
		600	
			Large-scale, organized elephant hunts staged in Europe
		400	Man begins to make artificial shelters from branches
		200	
Upper Pleistocene latest period of most recent epoch	**Middle Paleolithic** middle period of Old Stone Age		Neanderthal man emerges in Europe
		80	
		60	Ritual burials in Europe and Near East suggest belief in afterlife
			Woolly mammoths hunted by Neanderthals in northern Europe
		40	Cave bear becomes focus of cult in Europe
	Upper Paleolithic latest period of Old Stone Age		Cro-Magnon man arises in Europe
			Asian hunters cross Bering Land Bridge to populate New World
			Oldest known written record, lunar notations on bone, made in Europe
			Man reaches Australia
			First artists decorate walls and ceilings of caves in France and Spain
		30	Figurines sculpted for nature worship
		20	Invention of needle makes sewing possible
			Bison hunting begins on Great Plains of North America
Holocene present epoch	**Mesolithic** Middle Stone Age	10	Bow and arrow invented in Europe
			Pottery first made in Japan

(Last Ice Age)

▼ Four billion years ago   ▼ Three billion years ago

▲ Origin of the Earth (4.5 billion)   ▲ First life (3.5 billion)

ar left of each of the chart's four sections identifies the great geo-
ogical eras into which the earth's history is divided by scientists,
hile the second column lists the archeological ages of human his-
ory. The key dates in the rise of life and of man's outstanding
ccomplishments appear in the third column (years and events mentioned in this volume of The Emergence of Man appear in bold type).
The chart is not to scale; the reason is made clear by the bar below,
which represents in linear scale the 4.5 billion years spanned by the
chart—on the scaled bar, the portion relating to the total period of
known human existence (far right) is too small to be distinguished.

Geology	Archeology	Years B.C.	
Holocene (cont.)	Neolithic New Stone Age	9000	
			Sheep domesticated in Near East
			Dog domesticated in North America
		8000	Jericho, oldest known city, settled
			Goat domesticated in Persia
			Man cultivates his first crops, wheat and barley, in Near East
		7000	Pattern of village life grows in Near East
			Catal Hüyük, in what is now Turkey, becomes largest Neolithic city
			Loom invented in Near East
			Cattle domesticated in Near East
		6000	Agriculture begins to replace hunting in Europe
			Copper used in trade in Mediterranean area
	Copper Age		Corn cultivated in Mexico
		4800	Oldest known massive stone monument built in Brittany
		4000	Sail-propelled boats used in Egypt
			First city-states develop in Sumer
			Cylinder seals begin to be used as marks of identification in Near East
		3500	First potatoes grown in South America
			Wheel originates in Sumer
			Man begins to cultivate rice in Far East
			Silk moth domesticated in China
			Horse domesticated in south Russia
			Egyptian merchant trading ships start to ply the Mediterranean
			Pictographic writing invented in Near East
	Bronze Age	3000	Bronze first used to make tools in Near East
			City life spreads to Nile Valley
			Plow is developed in Near East
			Accurate calendar based on stellar observation devised in Egypt
		2800	Stonehenge, most famous of ancient stone monuments, begun in England
			Pyramids built in Egypt
		2600	Variety of gods and heroes glorified in Gilgamesh and other epics in Near East

Geology	Archeology	Years B.C.	
Holocene (cont.)	Bronze Age (cont.)	2500	Cities rise in the Indus Valley
			Earliest evidence of use of skis in Scandinavia
			Earliest written code of laws drawn up in Sumer
		2000	Minoan palace societies begin on Crete
			Use of bronze in Europe
			Chicken and elephant domesticated in Indus Valley
			Eskimo culture begins in Bering Strait area
		1500	Invention of ocean-going outrigger canoes enables man to reach islands of South Pacific
			Ceremonial bronze sculptures created in China
			Imperial government, ruling distant provinces, established by Hittites
		1400	Iron in use in Near East
			First complete alphabet devised in script of the Ugarit people in Syria
			Moses leads Israelites out of Egypt
	Iron Age	1000	Reindeer domesticated in Eurasia
			Phoenicians spread alphabet
		900	
		800	Use of iron begins to spread throughout Europe
			First highway system built in Assyria
			Homer composes Iliad and Odyssey
			Mounted nomads appear in the Near East as a new and powerful force
			Rome founded
		700	Etruscan civilization in Italy
			Cyrus the Great rules Persian Empire
		500	Roman Republic established
			Wheel barrow invented in China
		200	Epics about India's gods and heroes, the Mahabharata and Ramayana, written
			Water wheel invented in Near East
		0	Christian era begins

▼ Two billion years ago   ▼ One billion years ago

First oxygen-breathing animals (900 million) ▲   First animals to possess backbones (470 million) ▲   First men (1.3 million) ▲

Credits

Sources for the illustrations appear below. Credits from left to right are separated by semicolons, from top to bottom by dashes.

All photographs on pages 47 through 55 are by Mauro Pucciarelli, Rome, reproduced through the courtesy of Museo Gregoriano Etrusco, Vatican.

Cover—Painting by Michael A. Hampshire, background photograph by Marcella Pedone. 8—Mauro Pucciarelli, Rome, courtesy Museo Nazionale di Villa Giulia, Rome. 12, 13—John G. Ross. 14, 15—Maps by Rafael D. Palacios. 19—Leonard von Matt from Rapho Guillumette courtesy Museo Nazionale di Villa Giulia, Rome. 20—Courtesy Soprintendenza alle Antichità dell'Etruria, Florence; Dmitri Kessel courtesy Museo Civico, Bologna. 21—Leonard von Matt from Rapho Guillumette courtesy Museo Nazionale di Villa Giulia, Rome. 25—Courtesy The American Numismatic Society. 27 through 31—David Lees, reproduced through the courtesy of Prince Alessandro Torlonia and heirs of the Torlonia family. 32, 35—Leonard von Matt from Rapho Guillumette courtesy Museo Archeologico, Florence. 37—General Research and Humanities Division, The New York Public Library, Astor, Lenox and Tilden Foundations. 40—Mario Carrieri courtesy Museo Nazionale di Villa Giulia, Rome—Courtesy Arheoloski Muzej, Zagreb, Yugoslavia. 41—Leonard von Matt from Rapho Guillumette courtesy Museo Nazionale Tarquiniense, Tarquinia; Aldo Durazzi courtesy Soprintendenza alle Antichità dell'Etruria Meridionale, Rome (2)—Photo Bibliothèque Nationale, Paris. 44—Fotocielo. 45—Leonard von Matt from Rapho Guillumette. 56—Mauro Pucciarelli, Rome, courtesy Museo Archeologico, Florence. 59—Leonard von Matt from Rapho Guillumette courtesy Museo Nazionale di Villa Giulia, Rome. 60, 61—Drawing by Don Bolognese. 62—Leonard von Matt from Rapho Guillumette courtesy Museo Nazionale di Villa Giulia, Rome. 63—Leonard von Matt from Rapho Guillumette courtesy Museo Nazionale di Villa Giulia, Rome; Leonard von Matt from Rapho Guillumette courtesy Museo Archeologico, Florence. 64—Drawing by Don Bolognese. 66, 67—Mauro Pucciarelli, Rome. 69—Drawing by Don Bolognese. 70—Réunion des Musées Nationaux, Paris—Scala courtesy Museo Gregoriano Etrusco, Vatican. 71, 73—Leonard von Matt from Rapho Guillumette courtesy Museo Nazionale di Villa Giulia, Rome. 74—General Research and Humanities Division, The New York Public Library, Astor, Lenox and Tilden Foundations. 77 through 85—Courtesy Soprintendenza alle Antichità dell'Etruria Meridionale, Rome. 77—Leonard von Matt from Rapho Guillumette. 78—David Lees. 79—Mauro Pucciarelli, Rome. 80, 81—Leonard von Matt from Rapho Guillumette. 82, 83—Mauro Pucciarelli, Rome. 84, 85—David Lees. 86—Courtesy of the Trustees of the British Museum, London. 89, 90, 91—Leonard von Matt from Rapho Guillumette. 89—Courtesy Chiusi Museum. 90—Courtesy Chiusi Museum; Courtesy Museo Archeologico, Florence. 91—Courtesy Chiusi Museum; Courtesy Museo Nazionale Archeologico, Palermo. 92—Henry Groskinsky courtesy of the Trustees of the British Museum, London. 94—Mauro Pucciarelli, Rome, courtesy Museo Gregoriano Etrusco, Vatican—Leonard von Matt from Rapho Guillumette courtesy Museo Civico, Piacenza. 95—Adapted by Rafael D. Palacios from M. Pallottino, *The Etruscans,* translated by J. Cremona, 1955. Copyright M. Pallottino, 1955, reprinted by permission of Penguin Books, Ltd. 97, 101—Leonard von Matt from Rapho Guillumette courtesy Museo Nazionale di Villa Giulia, Rome. 102—David Lees courtesy Istituto di Etruscologia e di Antichità Italiche, Rome University. 103—Leonard von Matt from Rapho Guillumette courtesy Museo Nazionale di Villa Giulia, Rome. 104—Scala courtesy Museo Nazionale Tarquiniense, Tarquinia. 105—John G. Ross courtesy Museo Nazionale di Villa Giulia, Rome—Mauro Pucciarelli, Rome, courtesy Museo Nazionale di Villa Giulia, Rome. 106, 107—Courtesy Museo Nazionale di Villa Giulia, Rome, except upper right page 107, Courtesy of the Trustees of the British Museum, London. 106—Leonard von Matt from Rapho Guillumette—Mauro Pucciarelli, Rome; Leonard von Matt from Rapho Guillumette. 107—Mario Carrieri—Mauro Pucciarelli, Rome; Mario Carrieri; Leonard von Matt from Rapho Guillumette. 108—C. H. Krüger-Moessner courtesy Staatliche Antikensammlungen und Glyptothek, Munich. 110—Istituto Archeologico Germanico, Rome. 112, 113—Leonard von Matt from Rapho Guillumette courtesy Museo Nazionale Archeologico, Palermo. 115—Leonard von Matt from Rapho Guillumette courtesy Soprintendenza alle Antichità dell'Etruria Meridionale, Rome. 116—Courtesy of the Trustees of the British Museum, London. 118, 119—Al Freni courtesy Museum of Fine Arts, Boston. 120—Courtesy of the Trustees of the British Museum, London. 122, 123—Soprintendenza alle Antichità dell'Etruria Meridionale, Rome; Soprintendenza alle Antichità dell'Etruria, Florence—Alinari courtesy Museo Archeologico, Aquileia; far right, Soprintendenza alle Antichità dell'Etruria Meridionale, Rome. 125—Drawings by Nicholas Fasciano. 126—Leonard von Matt from Rapho Guillumette. 127—Courtesy Swedish Archeological Institute—Drawing by Nicholas Fasciano. 128—Leonard von Matt from Rapho Guillumette. 129—Drawing by Nicholas Fasciano, reproduced through the courtesy of the British School at Rome. 130—Dmitri Kessel courtesy Museo Nazionale di Villa Giulia, Rome. 132—Courtesy Swedish Archeological Institute. 135—Robert E. Lackenbach; From "An Inquiry into the Forgery of the Etruscan Terracotta Warriors in The Metropolitan Museum of Art" by Dietrich von Bothmer and Joseph V. Noble. Paper No. 11. Copyright 1961, The Metropolitan Museum of Art, New York. 136—Andreas Feininger. 137—From "An Inquiry into the Forgery of the Etruscan Terracotta Warriors in The Metropolitan Museum of Art" by Dietrich von Bothmer and Joseph V. Noble. Paper No. 11. Copyright 1961, The Metropolitan Museum of Art, New York—David Lees. 138—The Metropolitan Museum of Art, Bequest of Joseph H. Durkee, Gift of Darius Ogden Mills and Gift of C. Buxton Love, by Exchange, 1972. 141—Courtesy The Lerici Foundation, Rome. 143—Soprintendenza alle Antichità dell'Etruria, Florence. 147—Christopher Swann-Harbor Branch Foundation, Inc.; John G. Ross. 148—Julian Whittlesey—Map by Rafael D. Palacios after Jay Warren. 149—John G. Ross; Anna Marguerite McCann. 150—John G. Ross—Map by Rafael D. Palacios after Jay Warren. 151—Anna Marguerite McCann—Diagram by Rafael D. Palacios after John Stubbs. 152—Christopher Swann-Harbor Branch Foundation, Inc. 153—Anna Marguerite McCann.

Acknowledgments

For the help given in the preparation of this book, the editors are particularly indebted to David Ridgway, the Department of Archaeology, University of Edinburgh; Giovanni Scichilone, Assistant, Superintendency for South Etruria, Rome; and John B. Ward-Perkins, former Director of the British School at Rome. The editors also wish to express their gratitude to Francesca Boitani, Assistant, Graviscae excavations, Superintendency for South Etruria, Rome; Lionel Casson, Professor of Classics, New York University; Lucia Cavagnaro-Vanoni, The Lerici Foundation, Rome; Giuseppe Cocchi, Photo Archives, Superintendency for Etruria, Florence; Molly Cotton, the British School at Rome; Antoinette Decaudin, picture researcher, the National Museums of France, Paris; Caterina de Grassi, Photo Archives, Superintendency for South Etruria, Rome; the Department of Greek and Roman Antiquities, the British Museum, London; Francesca Fortunati, Etruscology Institute, Rome University; Bianca Gabrieli-Spantigati, Rome; Theodor Kraus, Director of the German Archeological Institute, Rome; Nino Lamboglia, Director of the Italian International Institute of Marine Archeology, and Anna Marguerite McCann, The Metropolitan Museum of Art, New York, Joint Directors of the Tuscan Port Project of the Atlantic

Foundation and the American Academy in Rome; Gabriella Lanzidei, Etruscology Institute, Rome University; Carlo M. Lerici, The Lerici Foundation, Rome; Guglielmo Maetzke, Superintendent, Superintendency for Etruria, Florence; Francesca Melis, Assistant, Etruscology Institute, Rome University; Marie Montambault, Department of Greek and Roman Antiquities, the Louvre Museum, Paris; Mario Moretti, Superintendent, Superintendency for South Etruria, Rome; Carl Eric Ostenberg, Director of the Swedish Institute in Rome; Kyle M. Phillips Jr., Associate Professor of Classical and Near Eastern Archeology, Bryn Mawr College, Pennsylvania; Duje Rendic-Miocevic, Director of the Archeological Museum, Zagreb, Yugoslavia; Mario Rinaldi, Photo Archives, Vatican Museums, Rome; Francesco Roncalli, Director of Etrusco-Italic Antiquities, Vatican Museums, Rome; Artur Svensson, Director of the Allhems Publishing Company, Malmö, Sweden; Anna Talocchini, Director, Superintendency for Etruria, Florence; Mario Torelli, Director, Graviscae excavations, Department of Archeology, Cagliari University, Italy; Prince Alessandro Torlonia, Rome; Germaine Tureau, Chief of the Photographic Documentation Service, the National Museums of France, Paris; Friedrich-Wilhelm von Hase, German Archeological Institute, Rome; Nancy M. Waggoner, Associate Curator of Greek Coins, American Numismatic Society, New York; Julian Whittlesey, the Whittlesey Foundation, Inc., New York.

Bibliography

General
Banti, Luisa, *Etruscan Cities and Their Culture.* University of California Press, 1973.
Bloch, Raymond, *The Etruscans.* Frederick A. Praeger, 1958.
Boethius, Axel, Carl Fries, et al., *Etruscan Culture.* Columbia University Press, 1962.
Dennis, George, *The Cities and Cemeteries of Etruria,* Vols. I and II. E. P. Dutton, 1907.
Deuel, Leo, *Flights into Yesterday.* St. Martin's Press Inc., 1969.
Heurgon, Jacques, *Daily Life of the Etruscans.* Macmillan Company, 1964.
MacKendrick, Paul, *The Mute Stones Speak.* Mentor Books, 1960.
Macnamara, Ellen, *Everyday Life of the Etruscans.* G. P. Putnam's Sons, 1973.
Pallottino, Massimo, *The Etruscans.* Penguin Books, 1975.
Richardson, Emeline, *The Etruscans.* University of Chicago Press, 1964.
Scullard, H. H., *The Etruscan Cities and Rome.* Cornell University Press, 1967.
Strong, Donald, *The Early Etruscans.* G. P. Putnam's Sons, 1968.
Von Vacano, Otto-Wilhelm, *The Etruscans in the Ancient World.* Indiana University Press, 1960.

Art
Bloch, Raymond, *Etruscan Art.* New York Graphic Society, 1965.
Boethius, Axel, and J. B. Ward-Perkins, *Etruscan and Roman Architecture.* Penguin Books, 1970.
Goldscheider, Ludwig, *Etruscan Sculpture.* Oxford University Press, 1941.
Hamblin, Dora Jane, *Pots and Robbers.* Simon and Schuster, 1970.
Hurlimann, Martin, and Massimo Pallottino, *The Art of the Etruscans.* Vanguard Press, 1955.
Jeppson, Lawrence, *The Fabulous Fakes.* Weybright and Talley, 1970.
The Metropolitan Museum of Art, "Etruscan Terracotta Warriors," Paper No. 6, 1937.
Meyer, Karl E., *The Plundered Past.* Atheneum, 1973.
Moretti, Mario, *New Monuments of Etruscan Painting.* Pennsylvania State University Press, 1970.
Skira, Albert, and Massimo Pallottino, *Etruscan Painting.* Editions Albert Skira, 1952.
Strom, Ingrid, *Problems Concerning the Origin and Early Development of the Etruscan Orientalizing Style.* Odense University Press, 1971.
Von Bothmer, Dietrich, and Joseph V. Noble, "An Inquiry into the Forgery of the Etruscan Terracotta Warriors." Paper No. 11, The Metropolitan Museum of New York, 1961.
Von Matt, Leonard, *Art of the Etruscans.* Harry N. Abrams, Inc., 1970.

History
Bloch, Raymond, *The Origins of Rome.* Frederick A. Praeger, 1969.
Boak, A., and W. Sinnigen, *A History of Rome to A.D. 565.* Macmillan Company, 1965.
Fell, R. A. C., *Etruria and Rome,* Cambridge University Press, 1924.
Harris, W. V., *Rome in Etruria and Umbria.* Clarendon Press, 1971.
Herodotus, *The History of Herodotus,* Vol. VI. Great Books of the Western World, Encyclopaedia Britannica, 1952.
Heurgon, Jacques, *The Rise of Rome.* University of California Press, 1973.
Livy, *The Early History of Rome.* Translated by Aubrey de Selincourt. Penguin Books, 1971.
Plutarch, *Lives.* Edited by Robert M. Hutchins. Great Books of the Western World, Encyclopaedia Britannica, 1952.

Religion
Bulfinch, Thomas, *Bulfinch's Mythology.* Thomas Y. Crowell Co., 1947.
Dumézil, Georges, *Archaic Roman Religion,* Vol. II. University of Chicago Press, 1970.
Weinstock, Stephan, "Martianus Capella and the Cosmic System of the Etruscans." *Journal of Roman Studies,* Vol. XXXVI. Society for the Promotion of Roman Studies, 1946.

Technology
Dilke, O. A. W., *The Roman Land Surveyors.* Barnes and Noble, Inc., 1971.
Judson, Sheldon, and Anne Kahane, "Underground Drainageways in Southern Etruria and Northern Latium." *Papers of the British School at Rome,* Vol. XXXI, 1963.
Lerici, Carlo Maurilio, *A Great Adventure of Italian Archaeology.* Lerici Editori, 1966.

Index

Numerals in italics indicate an illustration of the subject mentioned.